The HEART

of the

COURAGEOUS

Moving from Fear-Based to Love-Based Anger

Gary A. Kuzmich
and Harry A. Stewart, M.D.

Compass Global Media Group
11100 Ash St., Ste. 100
Leawood, KS 66211

Printed in the United States of America

First Edition: January 2012

ISBN: 10 Digit - 0984938702
        13 Digit - 978-0-9849387-0-4

The Feelings Inventory Chart for this book was adapted from the book, *Release from Powerlessness* by Dr. Linda Moore and is used by permission.

The Anger Quiz and Key in this book are used by permission from Ronald Potter-Efron, MSW, Ph.D. and Patricia Potter-Efron, M.S., authors of *Letting Go of Anger.*

The scale used in this book was developed by Richard Rahe, M.D. and Thomas Holmes, M.D. and is used by permission.

IMPORTANT NOTICE: The ideas, exercises and suggestions in this book are offered for informational and educational purposes only. This book is not presented as professional advice and cannot be used as a substitute for that advice. The co-authors and publisher disclaim any adverse effects claimed or presumed to result directly or indirectly from the use or application of the information contained in this book.

Other than voluntary testimonials, the scenarios, personal experiences and examples in this book are derived from many people who have shared their life stories with us. These descriptions do not describe any one person. Rather, each example is used only for clarity and editorial reasons. Names and potential identifying information have been changed to prevent any potential breach of anonymity.

DEDICATION

*To Betsy and Christy, and all those
who have been subjected to our unhealthy anger.*

ACKNOWLEDGEMENTS

*O*ur book has its roots in our marriages* when we became sick and tired of our unhealthy behavior toward our wives. In turn, they appreciated our changes and became our adamant supporters in the writing of this book. We are indebted to them for their countless hours of support, editing, suggestions, and rewrites.

We also give special thanks for the contributions and support of: Jessica Barnes, Tina Gaa-Pulley, Bryan Vignery LCPC, Monty Miller LCSW, Kristen Moeller, Russell Settle, M.D., Lisa Sewalson, Vesna Morris, Ryan Lefebvre, Erin Trivett, Dan Erickson Ph.D., Elsie Kuzmich, and Phil and Cathy Cosby. Our appreciation also extends to all of the participants in our Heart of the Courageous workshops from whom we learned and continue to learn.

—Gary Kuzmich
Harry Stewart, M.D.
January 20, 2012

TABLE OF CONTENTS

Chapter 3 - THE LAW OF SUPER-SATURATION:

FOREWORD

*H*eart of the Courageous: Moving from Fear-Based to Love-Based Anger speaks for itself; not just in its meaning but in the uniqueness of the title. This work is the result of living, studying, sharing, listening, examining, and reexamining life. I attended one of Gary and Harry's *Heart of the Courageous* seminars in 2007. I certainly didn't believe I had the rest of my life figured out but I felt as though I had a pretty firm grasp of my strengths and weaknesses. Then I learned about my anger. I say *my* anger because, as you will discover in this book, anger has many dimensions. I had confused being *enraged* with being angry. Furthermore, I learned that my anger wasn't entirely unproductive! There were several (understatement) examples of how I allowed anger to make me look like a horse's fanny in my life, and I still do today. Yet I also discovered that there were also several examples of when properly channeled anger was quite productive. In other words, I realized many significant accomplishments in my life were the result of anger... no horse's fanny involved.

So, grab onto this book with both hands and get ready to be angry in a new way. You've got two great men ready to take you for a ride.

—Ryan Lefebvre
Kansas City Royals Radio/TV Announcer
Author of *The Shame of Me: One Man's Journey to Depression and Back*

Preface: Authors' Journey

*A**nger is a gift. Are you kidding?!** This is the reaction most commonly given. Most people do not see anger as a gift but as a curse. They tend to think of anger as yelling, screaming, hitting, profanity or throwing things. Do any of these reactions seem familiar to you?

Maybe you are one of those who say, "I don't do those kinds of things. I don't get angry." Do you pout, maintain silence, avoid conflict, numb out or become sad? Everyone gets angry. Those are forms of anger. It's just a matter of where the anger goes; inside or out, imploding or exploding. Those who say they don't get angry are usually in denial about their anger and the hurt they are causing themselves and others. Unresolved anger will inevitably manifest itself at some point in our lives, creating even more pain.

Sometimes, it seems easier to just sweep anger under the rug rather than deal with it. It would be nice if handling anger was that simple. The good news is that, once anger is exposed, there is an opportunity to give it a healthy place in life. Learning to make anger an ally creates a deep sense of relief and even pride.

During our meeting for over six years as accountability partners, we discovered that both of us suffered from unhealthy anger and toxic shame. It was during these meetings that we acknowledged this premise: we didn't know what we didn't know. Not knowing what we did not know is in fact a "blind spot." Our blindness was revealed through discussion, stories, and similar behavior patterns.

These blind spots were actually the dishonesty unrecognized within ourselves.

We knew we had good hearts, yet our anger was hurting us and others. Our inappropriate outbursts or smoldering silences left an imprint on the lives of those closest to us. These reactions created a double-edged sword that cut the hearts of others as well as our own. We knew intuitively that we were not the only ones struggling to understand why anger was destroying our relationships. We started to see patterns and search out their origins.

DAMAGE DONE IN THE HEART CANNOT BE HEALED IN THE HEAD.

The more we met, read and discussed, the more we made sense out of the jigsaw puzzle of the past. We discovered something profound; damage done in the heart cannot be healed in the head. Both of us, being self-help gurus, were trying to heal everyone else but ourselves, just like a lawyer who doesn't have his own will and trust.

Finally, the pain was so intense that we decided to change and now intuitively knew it had to be from the inside out. Anger's curse would no longer rule our behaviors and destroy our relationships! Our friendship deepened, our expressions of anger changed, and our loved ones told us of their new found respect. Our wives even said they felt a sense of safety with us they had not known before. Gary's wife Christy stated, "I don't feel like I have to walk on eggshells when a conflict arises." Betsy, Harry's wife, indicated her relief that he was no longer blaming and attacking, but was willing to deal with the disagreement without resorting to unhelpful behaviors.

This sense of relief and dramatic improvement in our relationships was an unexpected gift. We also realized that others had to be struggling as well. The journey that appeared to be the road less traveled was, in actuality, a familiar road for many.

In the *Heart of the Courageous* workshop, our desire was to create an atmosphere where others could learn about their anger in a safe and healthy manner. We knew it took courage to make a heartfelt change. By participating in the workshop, men and women have been able to work through the maze of twisted thoughts and neurological patterns that have led to the same painful results. The positive outcome of the workshop became the impetus for writing this book.

We continue to meet each week. For us, understanding anger is a journey, not a destination. As we coach others through their struggle, we continue to heal. We have the opportunity to share our "medicine" with others who want to develop healthier ways of living through the gift of love-based anger.

—Gary and Harry

INTRODUCTION

*I*s *anger good or bad, right or wrong?* For most people, it is labeled
wrong. Anger acted out is unhealthy and destructive.

It is estimated that 65% of marriages are suffering through
physical abuse. Twenty-five percent of these include serious beatings
and 15-25% of these will end in homicide. Six million children are
abused. One out of four girls under the age of twelve and one out of
every six boys are sexually abused; 80% know their abusers. There
are 500,000 to 2,000,000 cases of elder abuse per year. Homicide is
four times higher in the US than any other nation.[1]

The truth is anger, purely as an emotion, is not right or wrong,
good or bad. Emotions are like colors; they are not good or bad. They
are not to be invalidated nor are they to be obeyed. Fear of anger, or
a belief that anger is wrong, stops us from responding effectively to
conflict. Conflict is inevitable in our relationships, yet many times
that very conflict generates anger.

When we begin to demystify anger, we learn that anger can actually
be a powerful, positive force. Anger comes in different styles, and is
experienced uniquely by each of us. Our inappropriate behavior and
negative feelings are neither who we really are nor who we want to
be. We are *not* our anger. As a result of the *Heart of the Courageous*
workshops, we have discovered that both men and women can, and
do, move past old beliefs and learned behaviors. Throughout this
book, you will discover through the 7 Laws of Anger, how to separate

---

[1] Violence against Women: A National Crime Survey Report, U.S. Department of Justice,
1994 and 1998

your anger from your behaviors. You will also learn how to separate your anger from your beliefs about yourself. You will no longer say, "I am an angry man/woman" but rather "I am a man/woman who gets angry." This shift, though subtle, makes a tremendous difference in how we view ourselves. Our anger becomes a behavior that we can learn to choose how to control.

Evidence indicates that everyone has anger, even those who say they don't. Anger is an emotion. An emotion can be defined as energy in motion and so anger is energy in motion. Anger will go somewhere if not given new meaning and direction.

ANGER WILL NOT JUST GO AWAY

Internalizing anger is usually a bittersweet experience. While, for the short-term, it can feel safe to avoid showing anger, long-term bitterness is erupting inside like an internal explosion. A child's first expression of anger, such as screaming or crying, is usually directed outward as a child knows no other way. If the child's anger is met with disapproval, criticism, yelling or shaming, the child will become adept at burying that anger by turning it inward. This is simply the child's learned response. On the outside, the child will display an appearance, or mask, that all is well. On the inside, uneasy feelings are stirring from wounds to the heart. It's a slow fade that gradually takes its toll on how grown-up children view themselves and respond to life's situations.

Each of us pays a high price for behaviors associated with inappropriate anger. The result may be alienated relationships with family and loved ones, distancing from co-workers, the loss of a job, a fight that ends in domestic violence, divorce, a trip to jail, or a psychosomatic illness that keeps a person stuck in perpetual victimhood. Many say, "There's no way out" or "Why bother?" Other people say, "Does it really make any difference?" Some are sick and tired of being sick and tired. Still others are caught in a "Catch-22," feeling anger but not knowing how to make it work for them in a healthy manner.

Expectations play a critical role in the way we express anger. Everyone has expectations which, sometimes, are unspoken or buried. Instead of talking about expectations, most of us hope that others will automatically understand our thoughts. Disappointment, sadness and outbursts are typical reactions to unmet expectations. Expectations can be premeditated resentments.

EXPECTATIONS CAN BE PREMEDITATED RESENTMENTS.

You, the reader, can learn to make anger your ally. You will discover the biology and psychology of anger, its numerous types and styles, and experience the pleasure of healthy anger. This book is for men, women, executives, wives, mothers, husbands, fathers, singles, ministers, rabbis, service workers, celebrities and sports figures. In short, it is for anyone wanting a better understanding of how to make anger a vital and healthy part of life.

The authors have used real life examples to help clarify conceptual language. The examples are a composite of the people with whom they have worked. Names have been changed to further ensure confidentiality.

Congratulations on picking up this book and making it this far! You have taken the first step in pursuing a better understanding of anger and learning how to make it fruitful in your life.

OUR STORIES

Harry's Story

I ***grew up in an alcoholic home,*** although I didn't know my father
was an alcoholic. What I did know was his anger. Although he was
usually irritable at any time of the day, he frequently became angrier
as the evening progressed. My mother's response taught me how to
hide my feelings in order not to aggravate
him. I guess she was trying to protect me from
his violent rampages. However, this hiding
and repression helped me survive his wrath.
At the same time I was learning to hide my
own anger, even from myself. I didn't know
it then, but he was modeling how to be angry
and what to be angry about. Simple mistakes

MY OWN
FEELINGS
WERE NEVER
ACKNOWLEDGED.

and human inadequacy put him into a rage. My own feelings were
never acknowledged. My father's devastating anger, criticism and
rejection created a sense of shame that left me feeling unworthy. His
anger was so intense, it felt toxic.

My way of coping was two-fold. On one hand, I became an
overachiever and people pleaser. It was an attempt to gain my father's
love and approval. On the other hand, because of shaming, I became
extremely self-conscious with low self-esteem, becoming masterful
at hiding my low opinion of myself. I portrayed to my family and the
world that I was a "hero." On the outside, I had the appearance of

calm and confidence. On the inside, I was tortured with self-doubt, anxiety and cynicism. My own repressed anger started to show after the death of my father when I was only thirteen. I began to exhibit some of my father's characteristics by yelling at my mother and brother. I was hyper-critical and cynical towards them. My Jekyll and Hyde personality was now clearly exposed.

I continued to lead this double life as an adult with very painful consequences. My private life was full of anger, mistrust, loneliness and fear. My relationships with women were especially troublesome. I married my wife to rescue her, rather than to be in a relationship of equals. I was determined to rescue her whether she needed or wanted it. I later realized that she experienced this as controlling and demeaning. When my efforts to save her were unsuccessful, my anger increased. My children later told me they became afraid of my anger and moodiness.

> MY JEKYLL AND HYDE PERSONALITY WAS NOW CLEARLY EXPOSED.

I had no concept that I was impaired. After all, I had gone to medical school and was a successful, well-respected psychiatrist. To the outside world, my family appeared to be "perfect." In private, I was a distant, critical and shaming husband and father, and a very lonely man. The cost of my behavior was high: two divorces, torn relationships with my children, continued personal feelings of guilt, shame, remorse and loneliness.

Gary's Story

grew up in a small town in upstate New York in an average, low to middle income family. I never realized how dysfunctional my family was until I was in college. To me, what I grew up with was normal. Everyone seemed to drink and everyone knew each other's business. I didn't realize that growing up in an alcoholic environment was abnormal and unhealthy. My father was a high-functioning, yet passive-aggressive alcoholic. My mother had been sick most of her life and needed a lot of health care. She was extremely anxious and nervous throughout my childhood; her illnesses made her protective and overbearing. When I would get angry my mother would say, "Oh, isn't it so cute when Gary can't get his way. Look at him pout or stomp his foot." I learned early in life that if I showed my feelings, I would be laughed at or told I shouldn't be angry.

Fighting, yelling, screaming and conflict were what I knew. I learned to place my fingers in my ears to block out the yelling and fighting. I would pound my head on my pillow while uttering moans louder than their fighting to help me go to sleep. I realized early in life to run and hide; whenever a fight broke out, I had to leave because I was so frightened. The loud yelling and screaming was shocking. Many fights ended in hitting and it was not unusual to see my father hauled away in a police car. How embarrassing and shaming! Even my friends would stand by and watch the freak show. I just wanted to run to the park and escape.

When I was twelve, my father left home and my brother went away to college. I became the surrogate husband and grew up way too fast. My mother often met her emotional needs through me. I had been a great student until then and as my home fell apart, my grades plummeted. I also became involved in anything that would help me avoid the prison I was in. I numbed my feelings through sports, girls, and alcohol. I found myself yelling and getting in more and more fights. I became my father; I expressed my anger just like he did.

A year after leaving, my father decided to return home when his girlfriend dumped him. I was just thirteen and now even more conflicted. In order to come home, he demanded my mother never mention his affair. If she did mention it, he would leave for good. I had to walk on eggshells and keep my mouth shut. No one said anything! The arguments between my parents continued.

WHAT MY FATHER AND MOTHER HAD DONE, IN WHAT SEEMED LIKE MODERATION, I WAS NOW DOING IN EXCESS.

Finally, I left home at eighteen. I vowed I would never yell or scream at my wife or children when I had a family. At twenty-seven I married and did my best to honor my wife. I had become an over-achiever and people pleaser. I continued to stuff my feelings, especially anger. By forty, I could no longer tolerate the pent-up emotions, and found myself raising my voice and recreating my own upbringing. I was passing down to my wife and children what I had learned. As a result, at 46, my marriage of twenty years was over. What my father and mother had done, in what seemed like moderation, I was now doing in excess. The damage was irreparable, ending in divorce and broken relationships with my children.

We all have a story. We recommend that you be courageously honest and write out your story. It is the beginning of a new path, one of increasing self-awareness and healthy changes.

CHAPTER 1

THE LAW OF REPRESSION:
"Who me, angry? Are you kidding?"

After eleven years, Jamie and Bill are experiencing fracture lines in their marriage. Bill's anger and criticism are increasingly frequent and hurtful. Jamie has tried to accept that the family debt and his workload are causing him to be more and more on edge. But her efforts to please him are not working and feelings of sadness and depression have been growing.

She does not yet recognize that Bill's anger and shaming are just like the way her father treated her during her childhood. And, just as in her childhood, she is burying her own hurt and anger to keep the peace. She is unaware that her antidote of repressing her pain creates an ineffective way to deal with the anger. She does not know that swallowing her feelings is a very temporary fix. Burying sadness, loneliness and anger causes a sideways movement to withdrawal, physical symptoms such as headaches, and even depression. The ensuing issue for Jamie is a growing sense of hopelessness.

Bill's anger is more obvious. Yet if you were to ask him about his anger, he would deny it or explain why it is warranted. Jamie's unrecognized anger is also having a serious effect.

The first step to changing unhealthy anger is to more completely identify the fact that it is present. We cannot heal or change what we do not first acknowledge. Let's find out what is true about you. Complete the evaluation form (Table 1), honestly sharing with yourself your reactions.

Let's get started finding out what is true about you now.

Table 1
Evaluation Form

Check all the areas that applied in the past or still apply today:

___I raise my voice when I get upset, irritated or angry.
___I may yell occasionally.
___I occasionally swear.
___I have raged but not always.
___I pout.
___I numb out.
___I shut down inside and remain quiet.
___I avoid further discussions.
___I make sarcastic comments.
___I steam on the inside and bite my tongue.
___I stare or look away.
___I change the subject or abruptly leave.
___I attack the other person.
___I may start an argument or even a fight.
___I defend myself and tell the other person that they are wrong.
___I do whatever it takes to calm the other person down.
___I get afraid.
___I feel hurt and disrespected.
___If in bed and I feel angry, I will turn my back on my partner and make it clear that they are on the outside.
___On the inside I hope that my partner will take some initiative but when they don't it drives my hurt even deeper.
___I tell the other person that they have issues and they need some help.
___I threaten to leave the house.
___I leave and don't mention when I will be back.
___I threaten by saying things like, I am moving out, or mention the "D" word.
___I cut off love and communication for hours and sometimes even days.
___I go read a self-help book on how to fix the situation.
___I call a friend and tell them how awful my partner has been to me.
___I wonder what others will think if they knew we fought and got angry.
___I throw things or sometimes break things.
___I have been known to be physically abusive and hit someone.
___I get angrier when I drink alcohol.
I medicate myself in other ways when I get angry.

___I have been in trouble with the law because of my anger.
___I take my anger out on other people who are not part of the problem.
___I get angry and then try to fix it by being nice.
___I do not tell even a close friend about my problems from anger.
___I try to please to prevent conflict with my partner.
___I feel sad or depressed when there is a conflict.
___I stuff my feelings.
___I sometimes have thoughts of revenge.

Now answer the following questions:

1. What causes me to get angry?

_____

_____

_____

2. What behaviors do I use to express my anger?

_____

_____

_____

After describing the symptoms of your anger and how you express it, answer these questions:

1. What, in my life, have I lost because of my anger?

_____

_____

_____

2. What has it cost me? [Think about all your relationships, job, health, finances, etc.]

_____

_____

_____

Spinning Wheel

"What goes up must come down; spinning wheel got to go round"[2] was a great song in the sixties. It is also the universal law of gravity. This concept applies to humans dealing with unpleasant feelings or traumatic events. When the pain of anger increases, it is commonly internalized by what is popularly called "stuffing." Like gravity, unresolved anger has its own law. What is stuffed must come out—it becomes like a hairball. It will spin round and round and eventually what was pushed down will come up.

YOU CANNOT HEAL OR CHANGE WHAT YOU DO NOT ACKNOWLEDGE[4]

All of us were taught through modeling to repress or stuff at least some of the unpleasant or painful events of our childhood. If we had been brave enough to act out our feelings, we were probably shamed, chastised or punished. We had no other choice but to repress our feelings. Repression can be defined as "the unconscious exclusion of painful impulses, desires, or fears from the conscious mind."[3] As part of the acknowledging process, the "What's Not Working?" sheet will help you identify areas in your life where your anger is exposed (Table 2). Remember, you cannot heal or change what you do not acknowledge.[4]

---

[2] David Clayton-Thomas, Blood, Sweat & Tears, 1969.
[3] Miriam Webster Dictionary
[4] The Passionate Heroic Zone, by Gary Kuzmich and Wayne McKamie, MSW, 2006.

Table 2
What's Not Working?

⊗   *Check the areas that currently apply in your everyday life.*
⊛   *Circle the areas that were once not working but now are working.*

○ Career
○ Marriage
○ Relationship
○ Children
○ Fear/anxiety
○ Parents
○ Siblings
○ Sickness
○ Stress
○ Financial pressures
○ Relationship with God
○ Anger/frustration
○ My weight
○ Too much time on my hands
○ Eating
○ Control/Controlled

○ Intimacy
○ Sex life
○ Thought life
○ Housing accommodations
○ Divorce
○ Divorce pending
○ Raising kids alone
○ Blending families
○ Dating
○ Loss of power
○ Restless
○ Financial success
○ Time pressures
○ Church/Synagogue
○ Exercise
○ Procrastination

Identifying "Not Working" areas will help you recognize potential blind spots for anger. For example, if you identified that your finances are not working then take the next step and ask, "What is not working with my finances?" You might say, "I don't have enough money to pay my bills", "My spouse doesn't follow our budget", "I am working two jobs and still cannot get ahead" or "My credit card debt is killing me." Asking defining questions develops clarity. Once you know what is not working, you are ready to identify the feelings that are associated with the problem. The journey to healthy anger begins with identifying what's not working and moves to revealing feelings. Remember, anger is often a secondary emotion.

REMEMBER, ANGER IS OFTEN A SECONDARY EMOTION.

Repression, pushing down thoughts or painful feelings, can be temporarily helpful until we are ready to deal with the pain. Repression can help us cope with events that are overwhelming or overpowering. It can help us remain strong, self-sufficient and cool under fire. It also helps us stay rational and perceptive during a time of crisis.

On the other hand, overuse of repression can have a significant cost. Usually, people are left with a limited variety of coping skills. At worst, stuffing has dramatic physical and psychological effects. Some of these effects are hypertension, heart attacks, depression, and anxiety as well as misdirected behavior. A particular cost of repression is the inability to recognize feelings in their free and undistorted state.

All of us have had life experiences which helped form who we are today. By the time we are pre-teens, we have developed a personality which includes a unique composite of hopes, desires, beliefs, fears and defenses. The larger part of this personality is out of sight, like an iceberg. What we see above the waterline is only a small part of the total personality. Below the waterline, the part we do not see is not right or wrong, good or bad. As with the Titanic, it was the unseen part of the iceberg that sank the ship. In a similar way, the unrecognized parts of our self can create a significant tear in the fabric of our life.

THE UNRECOGNIZED PARTS OF OUR FEELINGS NEED RECOGNITION AND VALIDATION.

You also cannot heal what you do not feel. The unrecognized parts of our feelings need recognition and validation. There are reasons why we are oversensitive, insensitive or numb. Again, feelings are not right or wrong. They are like colors or vegetables; some we may like more than others. They are not to be invalidated nor are they to be obeyed. We are more than our feelings. We may have been taught that feelings show weakness. We may have been told, "Suck it up", "Don't be a baby", "Real men don't cry", "You are just too sensitive", "Silly girl", "Get serious" or "Quit behaving like a princess." Messages like these only serve to suppress our feelings until we feel safe again. They create a sense of powerlessness and fear of intimacy.

A dilemma is caused by the seeming demands of home and society that we be independent, powerful and self-sufficient. And yet, how can we be truthful, compassionate, and respectful with others when our subconscious is told to be more powerful? Intimacy, for so many equates to losing power. Showing feelings threatens our self-image and proves us powerless. "Real people", often defined as "successful people," must stay in control and not show feelings. Their feelings must stay buried in order to maintain a distorted self-image that resonates with, "I must not lose my power... I cannot remove my mask, for if I do I will feel exposed and powerless!"

The common message for men is to focus on tasks and work, while for women it is to focus on relationships. Men usually function as protectors, hunters and providers. They tend to believe, either subconsciously or consciously, that their role is to solve problems, work for their worth and protect women. Women generally feel their relationships through nurturing, mothering and creating a home. It is predictable that when men are asked, "How do you feel?" the answer will be one of the following: "I don't know", "Good", "Great", "I think I feel...", "Okay", "What do you mean?" a sarcastic comment, or a blank look. Men often have a difficult time identifying their feelings. Women tend to talk out their feelings and therefore seem more in touch with a variety of emotions. Yet even women repress certain feelings, especially anger; they have difficulty identifying some feelings and separating those feelings from their true selves.

To help you have a clearer picture of your feelings, complete the following worksheet.

Table 3
Feelings

Circle the words that describe how you are feeling. Move quickly through the words checklist without thinking them. In essence, don't think your feelings, just feel them.

apprehensive	reverence	rage	infuriated	bummed	melancholy
terror	doubtful	furious	irritated	depressed	gloomy
leery	inadequate	angry	accosted	sorrow	dismay
uneasy	scared	enraged	indignant	downcast	mournful
anxiety	awe	hot	pissed	low	shameful
frightened	paranoid	hostile	fury	discontent	timid
panic	alarmed	uptight	resentment	woeful	disappointed
spooked	skeptical	inflamed	irate	uncertain	unhappy
fearful	afraid	annoyed	wrath	failure	regret
mistrust		upset	provoked	dejected	blue
afraid		animosity		brooding	somber
horror		mad		worried	helpless

powerless	weak	vengeance	animosity	down	overpowered
dependent	incompetent	bitter	bitterness	overtaken	pushed
lost	crippled	hostile	envy	captive	tyrannized
exhausted	resourceless	disfavor	detest	misused	used
feeble	spent	dislike	loathing	trampled	crossed
vulnerable	abandoned	adverse	despise	trodden	mistreated
defenseless	inefficient	abhorance	disaffection	afflicted	subdued
destitute	depleted	hateful		burdened	pressured
impotent		spite		crushed	
defeated		resentment		persecuted	

failure	unsatisfied	happy	glad	loving	adulation
unfulfilled	discouraged	gaiety	mirth	passion	admiration
discontent		freaked-out	jazzed	desiring	affectionate
disillusioned		mellow	pleasure	concern	adoring
disenchanted		exuberant	turned-on	appreciation	adoring
failed		jubilant	elated	rejoiceful	empathy
downcast		terrific	contentment	caring	togetherness
unhappy		elation	triumphant	befriended	
let-down		spirited	wonderful	infatuation	

Now, write the following words in the large boxes above (left to right):
Fear, Anger, Sadness, Powerlessness, Hate, Oppression, Disappointment, Joy, Love

Write the total number of circled feelings for each category in the small boxes. Below, total the number of love and joy feelings, non-love and non-joy feelings, and all feelings.

Love & Joy	☐
Non-Love & Joy	☐
Total	☐

Adapted from Dr. Linda L. Moore's book *Release from Powerlessness*

Completing the feelings checklist, without judging your responses, will validate the existence of your feelings. This is the beginning of finding the energy and power contained in emotion. We can now begin to shape this energy by validating anger, rather than fighting or denying it. Removing beliefs that feelings are right or wrong allows the discovery of blind spots.

Fable of the Indian Boy

A young Indian boy went to the wise old chief for help. "Chief, I seem to have two wolves at war in my head. The black wolf is angry, critical and constantly upset with me. The other wolf, a white one, is loving, supportive and affirming. Some days, the black wolf seems to be stronger. Other days, the white wolf seems stronger. Can you tell me which one will win?" The wise old chief answered, "The one you feed the most."

This story helps us understand the truth about our feelings. The black wolf represents our non-love and non-joy feelings. The white wolf represents our love and joy feelings. They often are at war within us. As the Chief stated, we get to choose which feelings we feed. What feelings do you feed? Which wolf is winning the war in your head?

Feelings can be compared to the lights on the dashboard of your vehicle. They alert us that something needs attention. We are free to ignore, react or respond to the warnings. However, the wise response is to pay attention to the light, ask questions, seek information, and take your vehicle to a mechanic for assistance. The light could be about a simple fuse that needs replacing or it might indicate a more serious problem, such as a needed engine repair. Reacting to our feelings without the facts keeps us in an unproductive cycle. Just as with our car, our response to a situation might lead to a regrettable malfunction or break down. The price of not paying attention to our feelings can be costly.

THE PRICE OF NOT PAYING ATTENTION TO OUR FEELINGS CAN BE COSTLY.

Let's look for a moment at the difference between price and cost. We may choose to buy something that is inexpensive based on the price, only to find that the product did not perform as desired. Purchasing a cheaper model bicycle or cheaper clothing can result in dissatisfaction in a short time. Thinking I can only afford to buy inexpensive clothes may seem cheaper, but be costly in the long run.

Feelings, too, have a price and a cost. I can choose to handle my anger inexpensively by continuing to react in the same hurtful ways without admitting the cost. The wiser choice would be to admit the presence of my costly, untamed anger and seek its repair.

YOU ARE MORE THAN YOUR ANGER.

Feelings of anger can seem to dictate angry behavior, but you are more than your anger! Anger is a normal part of life, and the behavior associated with it can be shown in healthy rather than hurtful ways.

Two Voices, One Body

Much research has substantiated the developmental process of the inner child. John Bradshaw[5] and Charles Whitefield[6] have, among others, written books describing the inner child. We see development of the inner child as progressing into a private and public self.

On a scale of 1-10, we believe children are born a 10. They are innocent and perfectly at peace with themselves. Although children are born a 10, they do not always behave this way. Even in the best of families, children are confronted with real-world problems; children develop defense mechanisms in order to cope with these situations. A child instinctively develops self-protection tools in order to survive, regardless of whether they understand this process. Their resulting behaviors will often appear to be less than a 10, such as the "terrible twos," threes, or even teens.

CHILDREN NEED TO BE TAUGHT TO SEPARATE ANGRY FEELINGS FROM ANGRY BEHAVIOR.

An unborn child of four months will attempt to pull back when an instrument is introduced into the uterus during an abortion. Even the unborn child instinctively uses visceral reflexes to avoid the danger. At this early age the child already seems to have a primal awareness of the need for protection.

As a child develops thoughts and emotions, he or she will learn other ways to cope with and avoid painful events. Their need to protect

[5] John Bradshaw, *Homecoming: Reclaiming and Championing Your Inner Child*
[6] Charles Whitfield, *Healing the Child Within*

themselves, and yet not upset caregivers, soon leads to the development of a private self and a public self. Our private self may not feel like a 10 and our public self will often not behave like a 10.

Children instinctively protect themselves. They do this physically through a fight or flight reaction. They do it emotionally with a variety of psychological defense mechanisms. Anger alerts them to physical and psychological threats.

WHEN ANGER IS DENIED, IT BECOMES SUPPRESSED OR EVEN REPRESSED.

Even in the best of families, a child will experience wounds when they make efforts toward independence and self-control. As a child we have little control over the adults who shape our sense of self. This leads to a natural splitting of one's self in order to survive. A child develops the outward, public self to adapt and conform to the expectations and demands of caregivers. The private, inner-self goes into hiding to keep from expressing resistance or disagreement. This separation process is an understandable and necessary need for self-protection.

As a child develops, anger becomes a natural emotion that helps to alert them to physical and psychological danger. Anger becomes a guardian of our self-esteem even when we don't understand. When a child has the freedom to feel their anger they are allowed to separate angry feelings from angry behavior. When anger is denied, it becomes suppressed or repressed with significant consequences.

When anger is repressed, our soul is distressed. This distress adds to the self-surviving creation of the public and private self. This anger is fear-based. When anger is fear-based, it can become destructive and harmful to one's self and others.

Children need to know that their anger is natural and normal. Having anger is no different than breathing. Labored breathing, like anger, is a signal of an unseen cause. When anger is love-based, however, it is a magnificent, protective gift. It is the essence of courage to deliberatively choose to move from fear-based anger to love-based anger.

WHEN ANGER IS LOVE-BASED, IT IS A MAGNIFICENT, PROTECTIVE GIFT.

Love and fear can work together in a healthy manner. Take the real life example of the mother who saw her son trapped under his '64 Chevy Impala.[7] She was motivated by fear to save him. She was motivated by love to lift the car that had fallen on his chest. The car was the threat; her anger was directed in a powerful way to lift the car and protect her son. Her son could then be pulled away by neighbors. After the incident, she did not know how she lifted the car. The mother's reaction was an immediate response that seemed to be motivated by fear and love.

Understanding anger can be healthy and helpful is a new belief. When we are taught that anger is wrong or negative, the belief is tainted and fear-based.

In the previous story, the mother's anger was neither right nor wrong; it was love-based. It is the inappropriate behaviors associated with anger that are right or wrong, not the anger!

When a child becomes angry and strikes out toward another child, a caregiver's response will determine what the child learns about anger. A loving response from the caregiver will teach the child

[7] Cecil Adams, "The Straight Dope," *The Chicago Reader*, January 20, 2006, 5.

that the anger is okay but the behavior is inappropriate. A response of fear or anger by the caregiver will create fear and shame in the child. This will, in turn, promote repression.

When our anger is repressed, our behavior will manifest itself in unhealthy ways. The child innately knows that their anger is okay but has now been taught that their anger and behavior are the same. The belief system becomes, "I am my anger." Therefore, when anger is labeled as bad, wrong and negative and my behaviors are bad, wrong and negative, then I must be bad, wrong and negative.

BETTER KEEP YOURSELF CLEAN AND BRIGHT, YOU ARE THE WINDOW THROUGH WHICH YOU MUST SEE THE WORLD.

We survive this dilemma by creating a public and private self. There is a saying, "Better keep yourself clean and bright, you are the window through which you must see the world."[8] If you do not see yourself as a 10, will the world be seen as a 10? Repression will become self-sustaining. Use the following worksheet to identify examples of repression in your life (Table 4).

---

[8] George Bernard Shaw, 1856-1950.

Table 4
Evidence of Repression

Do you repress your anger? **Check** *the following statements that apply:*

- ☐ When I get angry, I don't get over it.
- ☐ I feel frustrated, disappointed or irritable much of the time, but I just don't ever get angry.
- ☐ I am sarcastic or cynical about myself, others, or the world around me.
- ☐ I often go overboard with my teasing.
- ☐ I am depressed frequently for long periods of time.
- ☐ I seem to get angry all of the time.
- ☐ I feel powerless about my life.
- ☐ I feel guilty when I get angry.
- ☐ I feel ashamed when I get angry.
- ☐ I withdraw or remove myself emotionally when I am hurt or angry.

CHAPTER 2

THE LAW OF AGGRESSION;
What's Wrong with Being Aggressive?

Types of Anger: Explosive and Implosive

Talking about types of anger helps to demystify them. It is a necessary step for change.

Anger is often viewed as being aggressive and easy to see. However, the aggressive form of anger can be internal or external – or both.

Anger can be classified into two general types, explosive and implosive. These two types describe the initial direction – outward or inward – of the anger. Both types result in a sudden release of energy with a potentially damaging outcome. Both are created by fear and the need for self-protection. When we are threatened, we instinctively fight back, pull away or bury feelings.

Anger that is explosive is what most of us think of when we consider "anger." A person with explosive anger might walk around with a sword in its sheath, but readily draws that sword and starts slashing. Explosive anger can also be compared to a grenade, or in today's terms, an individual explosive device (IED). This kind of anger can manifest itself in sudden, impulsive, or even addictive behaviors.

Implosive anger, while often difficult to detect or see, is just as damaging in its total effect. Imploded anger redirects the energy of anger internally rather than externally. Implosive anger is often masked by avoidance of conflict. It is also masked as withdrawing, numbing out, sarcasm, hiding, sadness, depression, and sneaky behavior. We have found that implosive anger can even be more destructive than explosive anger because it is hidden for so long before showing its ugly and explosive head.

Styles of Anger

Various styles of anger can be identified within these two basic types of anger. The following chart modifies the thoughts and work of Potter-Efron, a husband-wife team who are widely written and professionally respected in the field of psychology (Table 5)[9] These styles are descriptions of various forms that the directed energy of anger may take.

More important than these descriptions is the understanding of our own anger responses. Increased understanding, in turn, will move us in the direction of more effective choices.

---

[9] Potter-Efron, Ronald and Patricia Potter, Efron, *Letting Go of Anger: The 10 most common anger styles and what to do about them*, pp 6 – 12.

Table 5
10 Styles of Anger

Explosive

Predictable: Grenade or IED

1. Sudden anger (impulsive, immediate)

2. Shame-based anger (hidden, poor self-image)

3. Deliberate anger (calculated, planned)

4. Addictive anger (self-fulfilling)

Unpredictable is Predictable: Long Fuse or Gotcha

5. Habitual anger (learned, repeated)

6. Moral anger (judgmental, self-righteous)

7. Hate (hardened resentment)

Implosive

Unpredictable: Camouflaged

8. Anger avoidance (denial, stuffing)

9. Sneaky anger (silent aggression)

10. Paranoid anger (hyper-suspicious)

Quiz to Identify Styles of Anger

Potter-Efron's quiz is intended to identify a person's anger style; your answers will help clarify what styles you tend to exhibit when you feel angry (Table 6). Check each box that applies to you. After checking the statements that apply, follow the directions to summarize your answers.

Example: if you checked numbers 1 and 2 in the first section, you would put "2" in that first, lower section labeled "1-3". This would mean you have 2 out of 3 of that particular anger style. If you checked numbers 4, 5, and 6 in the next section of responses, you would put "3" in the summary line down below.

Notice that the questions are separated into sets of three. Each set is about one anger style.

Table 6
Anger Quiz

Check the boxes next to the statements that apply to you:

☐ 1. I try to never get angry.
☐ 2. I get really nervous when others are angry.
☐ 3. I feel I'm doing something bad when I get angry.
☐ 4. I tell people I'll do what they want, but then I often forget.
☐ 5. I say things like, "Yeah, but…" and "I'll do it later."
☐ 6. People tell me I must be angry, but I'm not sure why.
☐ 7. I get jealous a lot, even when there is no reason.
☐ 8. I don't trust people very much.
☐ 9. Sometimes it feels like people are out to get me.
☐ 10. My anger comes on really fast.
☐ 11. I act before I think when I get angry.
☐ 12. My anger goes away very quickly after I explode.
☐ 13. I get very angry when people criticize me.
☐ 14. People say I am easily hurt and oversensitive.
☐ 15. I get angry when I feel bad about myself.
☐ 16. I get mad in order to get my way.
☐ 17. I try to scare others with my anger.
☐ 18. I can pretend to be very mad when I'm really OK.
☐ 19. Sometimes I get angry just for the excitement or action.
☐ 20. I like the strong feelings that come with my anger.
☐ 21. My anger takes over and I go out of control.
☐ 22. I seem to get angry all the time.
☐ 23. I just can't break the habit of getting angry a lot.
☐ 24. I get mad without thinking—it just happens.
☐ 25. I become very angry when I defend my beliefs and opinions.
☐ 26. I feel outraged about what others try to get away with.
☐ 27. I always know I'm right in an argument.
☐ 28. I hang onto my anger for a long time.
☐ 29. I have a hard time forgiving people.
☐ 30. I hate people for what they've done to me.

Total the number of statements that applied to you from each group of three questions

Questions	Total that apply	Anger Style
1-3	_____	Anger Avoidance
4-6	_____	Sneaky Anger
7-9	_____	Paranoid Anger
10-12	_____	Sudden Anger
13-15	_____	Shame-based Anger
16-18	_____	Deliberate Anger
19-21	_____	Addictive Anger
22-24	_____	Habitual Anger
25-27	_____	Moral Anger
28-30	_____	Hate

What can you learn from this quiz? A positive response of two or more in a set of statements indicates that it is one of your anger styles. A single response in a category suggests it is a style you may use, but less frequently.

Now read the following descriptions of each style from Potter-Efron's book, Letting Go of Anger: The 10 Most Common Anger Styles and What to Do about Them. A description of a style may seem familiar to you. This may suggest that it is also one of your styles.

Anger Avoidance (1 – 3)

Sally says she'll meet Joe for lunch, but she doesn't show up. It's the third time in a row, but is Joe angry? Of course not! He never gets mad, he says. Joe would feel like a bad person if he got angry.

Anger avoiders don't like anger much. Some avoiders are afraid of their anger as well as the anger of others. Anger seems too scary; these people are scared of losing control if they get mad and of letting out the monster inside them. Other avoiders think that it's just plain bad to be angry. They've learned to say comments like, "Only dogs get mad" and "Be nice, don't be angry." They hide from their anger because they want to be liked and fit a prescribed role that does not allow anger.

Anger avoiders gain the sense of being a good or nice person because they don't get mad. This helps them feel safe and calm.

Anger avoiders have problems, though. They often don't feel anger even when something is wrong, so anger doesn't help them. Also, they can't be assertive because they feel too guilty when they say what they want. Too often the result is that they end up being walked on by others.

Sneaky Anger (4 – 6)

The church ladies are calling again. They want Ruth to make sandwiches for 100 people next week at the social. Ruth has other plans, but she says OK. The day of the picnic comes and no Ruth. She just forgot, she explains when they call, and now there isn't time. Too bad, but they'll have to find someone else.

Anger sneaks never let others know when they are angry. In fact, they sometimes don't even know how angry they are. But the anger comes out "sideways" when they forget things a lot. Sometimes they say "Yeah, but..." over and over instead of doing anything or they simply sit around and frustrate everybody in their families. When others get mad at them, anger sneaks can look hurt and innocent. They ask, "Why are you getting mad at me? "I haven't done anything." That's the problem. Since they are angry, anger sneaks don't do what they are asked or told to do. In fact, they don't tell anybody about their resentments.

Anger sneaks gain a sense of control over their lives when they frustrate others. By doing little or nothing, or by putting things off, they thwart other people's plans. In addition, they can be angry without having to admit their actions or lack thereof. "It's not my fault you expect too much from me," they say.

Sneaky anger creates problems, though. The biggest issue is anger sneaks lose track of their own wants and needs. They don't follow through on what they have promised or need to do to be healthy, successful individuals. True, they keep from meeting the expectations of others but then what? They don't know what to do with their lives. This leads to boredom, frustration and unsatisfying relationships.

Paranoid Anger (7 – 9)

Howard loves Millie, but he's scared he'll lose her. That's why he follows her everywhere. That's why he asks her all those questions. He flies into a rage whenever she even glances at another man. Howard's so jealous, he's driving Millie crazy. She told him that if he can't control his temper she's going to break off their relationship.

But jealousy isn't Howard's only problem. He's also suspicious a lot of others' motives. He doesn't trust many people and, sometimes, he wonders what others are going to do next to hurt him. Frequently he accuses others of being out to "screw" him, but he knows it isn't true.

This is paranoid anger, which is most commonly expressed as hyper-suspiciousness. It occurs when someone feels irrationally threatened by others. Those who are hyper-suspicious see aggression everywhere. They are certain that others will want to take what is "theirs." They expect that others will attack them physically or verbally. Because of this belief, they spend much time jealously guarding and defending what they think is theirs—the love of a partner (real or imagined), money, or other valuables.

People with paranoid anger give their anger away. They think everybody else is angry instead of acknowledging their own anger or rage. Since they think others are attacking them, they believe they must defend themselves. They have found a way to get angry without guilt. Their anger is disguised as self-protection.

Paranoid anger is expensive, though. Paranoids are insecure. They trust nobody. Worse, they have poor judgment because they confuse their own feelings with those of others. They see their own anger in the eyes and words of their friends, mates and coworkers. That leaves them (and everybody else) confused.

Sudden Anger (10 – 12)

Martha is furious. Her mother has finally set a date for her to move out of the house. How dare she! Martha's instantly enraged. She's yelling and throwing things, beating her fists on the wall. Her rage only lasts a few minutes, but by then her mom is crying and running out the door.

People with sudden anger are like thunderstorms on a summer day; they zoom in from nowhere, blast everything in sight and then vanish. Sometimes it's only thunder and lightning, a big show that soon blows over. But often people get hurt, homes are broken up, and relationships are damaged that will take a long time to repair.

People with sudden anger gain a surge of power. They release all their feelings, giving them a sudden rush of relief. They "let it all hang out," for better or worse.

Loss of control is a major problem with sudden anger. People with sudden anger can be dangerous to themselves and others; they may get violent. They usually say and do things they later regret, but by then it's too late to take it all back.

Shame-based Anger (13 – 15)

Mary's husband Bill drives to the theater to pick her up from a movie. When he gets to the theater, he forgets to ask her how she enjoyed the movie. "Well, that's proof he doesn't love me," she thinks to herself. "If he cared, he'd want to know if I had a good time. Boy, does that burn me up!"

People who need a lot of attention, or are very sensitive to criticism, often develop shame-based anger. The slightest criticism or brush off touches their shame. Unfortunately, they don't like themselves very much. They feel unworthy, not good enough, broken and unlovable. So when somebody ignores them or says something negative, they take it as proof that the other person dislikes them as much as they dislike themselves. But that validation of their own poor self-image gets them really angry, so they lash out. They think: "You made me feel awful, so I'm gonna hurt you back."

People with shame-based anger play hot potato with their shame. They try to get rid of their shame by blaming, criticizing and ridiculing others. Their anger helps them feel protected against anybody they think shamed them. The sufferers of this type of anger avoid their own feelings of inadequacy by shaming others.

Raging against others to hide shame doesn't work very well. Those with shame-based anger end up attacking the people they love, suffering broken or strained relationships. Meanwhile, they continue to be oversensitive to insults because of their poor self-image. Their anger and loss of control only makes them feel worse about themselves.

Deliberate Anger (16 – 18)

William wants sex tonight. His wife says no. He starts to pout and then accuses her of being cold. He looks awfully angry, almost out of control. Odd, though, that when his wife gives in and says she'll go to bed with him, his anger vanishes. How can someone be terribly angry one second and totally calm the next?

Deliberate anger is planned. People who use anger this way usually know what they're doing. They aren't really emotional about their anger, at least not at first. They like controlling others and the best way they've discovered to do that is with anger and, sometimes, violence. Power and control are what people gain from deliberate anger. Their goal is to get what they want by threatening or overpowering others.

Deliberate anger may work for a while. However, this style usually breaks down in the long run. Other people don't like being bullied, and they eventually figure out ways to leave or get back at the bully.

Addictive Anger (19 – 21)

Melinda is a "rageaholic." She feels depressed a lot, bored with her life. Once in a while, she gets bent out of shape and really blows up. You know what she told us, "I really feel alive when I get into a fight; that adrenaline rush is great. It's the only time I feel really excited."

Some people want or need the strong feelings that come with anger. They like the intensity of the anger even if they don't like the trouble that the emotion causes them. Their anger is much more than a bad habit; it provides emotional excitement. Anger isn't fun, but it is powerful. Rageaholics look forward to the anger "rush," also known as the emotional "high". Since anger addicts gain a surge of intensity and emotional power when they explode, these people will have trouble giving up their anger. They feel alive and full of energy with their emotional outburst. Like others who cling to gambling, cocaine, or risk-taking behaviors, their lives seem dull without these periods of tremendous feeling.

Addictions are inevitably painful and damaging. Anger addiction is no exception. Anger addicts don't learn other ways to feel good, so they become dependent upon their anger. They pick fights just to get high on anger. And, since they need intensity, their anger takes on an all-or-none pattern that creates more problems than it solves.

Habitual Anger (22 – 24)

Ralph is really getting tired of being angry with his kids, but he just can't stop. Every night, like clockwork, he comes home and starts screaming at them. He's angry before he even gets in the door. When the kids give him that "Oh, there he goes again" look, he gets even angrier.

Those with habitual anger have created a nonproductive habit. Such people find themselves getting angry often, usually about small things that don't bother others. They wake up grumpy and they go through the day looking for fights. People with habitual anger tend to look for the worst in everything and everybody. They usually go to bed pissed off about something; they might even have angry dreams. Their angry thoughts set them up for more and more arguments. They can't seem to quit being angry, even though they are unhappy.

Habitually angry people do gain predictability. They always know what they feel (because their main feeling is anger). Life may be lousy, but it is known, safe and steady.

Yet, people with habitual anger get trapped in their emotional baggage; anger runs their lives. They can't get close to the people they love and form healthy relationships because their anger keeps them at a distance.

Moral Anger (25 – 27)

Joan is a crusader. She's always fighting for a cause. Today it's one thing and tomorrow another. But whatever the situation is, she's absolutely certain she is on the side of justice. She feels furious at those who think differently than she does. She wears the cloak of righteousness as if it were designed by her personal tailor. Joan doesn't see her attitude as self-righteousness; she has her own catalog of what is right or wrong.

Morally angry people think they have a right to be angry when others have broken a rule. They judge the offenders as bad, evil, wicked and sinful. The wrong-doers should be scolded, maybe punished. They have to be brought back in line. People with this anger style feel outraged about what those "bad" people are doing. The crusaders say they aren't angry for themselves. They feel they have the right to fight to defend their beliefs, claiming moral superiority.

Self-righteous people gain the sense that their anger is for a good cause; they don't feel guilty when they get angry. Indeed, they often feel superior to others even in their anger. "Yes, I'm angry," says the crusader, "but I've got a good reason. I'm defending a good cause, so I have a right to get mad." These anger sufferers would rather be right than happy.

These people struggle with "black-and-white thinking," which means they see the world too simply. They fail to understand people who are different than themselves and they often have rigid ways of thinking and accomplishing goals. Another problem with this anger style is crusading. Crusaders attack every problem or difference of opinion with moral anger when compromise or understanding might be more successful.

Hate (28 – 30)

Mona is going through the world's messiest divorce. She's on the stand now, testifying against her husband. But look at her face; you can see the hate in her eyes. She would say anything to hurt him, whether it's true or not.

Hate is hardened resentment. This anger style occurs when someone decides that another person is totally evil or bad. Forgiving the other person seems impossible. Instead, the hater decides to despise the offender. Hate starts as anger that never finds resolution. The anger eventually becomes resentment, followed by true hatred which can continue indefinitely. Haters often obsess about ways they can punish the offender. Sometimes, they act on those ideas.

People who hate hold onto the feeling that they are innocent victims. They create a world of enemies to fight, attacking these foes with great vigor and enthusiasm.

However, hatred causes serious damage over time. Haters can't let go or get on with life. They become bitter and frustrated. Their lives become mean, small and narrow.[10] But not all resentments become hatred. Some people just stew over past offenses and only talk about them when provoked. Still, resentments contribute to feelings of depression, despair and misery. Resentment is like swallowing poison hoping the other person dies.

RESENTMENT IS LIKE SWALLOWING POISON HOPING THE OTHER PERSON DIES.

Your Anger Style

These classifications of anger will clarify your particular anger style(s). If you feel disheartened by what you have learned about your anger styles, you are most likely judging yourself. Guilt or remorse is a common feeling when learning about anger styles. Remember, they are not right or wrong. Acknowledging your particular anger style(s) creates the awareness that you are accountable for your expressions of anger.

Separating our feelings of anger from the way we express our anger is critical to changing harmful patterns. The ineffective expressions of anger vary from mild to severe: from a scowl to verbal and physical abuse. Recognizing that feelings of anger are neither

[10] Potter-Efron, Ronald and Patricia Potter-Efron, *Letting Go of Anger: The 10 most common anger styles and what to do about them,* (New York, Barnes & Noble Books 1995), 6-12.

right nor wrong does not excuse our behavior. How we express anger is a choice.

Of course, abusive anger is illegal and immoral. Physical, sexual, verbal and emotional abuses are all inappropriate expressions of anger. This alone is ample reason to preempt inappropriate expressions of anger.

Where and How You Learned Your Anger Styles

Most expressions of anger are learned from observing or experiencing parents, siblings or others close to us. In addition, young children today are exposed to violent expressions of anger through television, video games and sporting events. The subtle message is, "Do what your feelings dictate to get what you want." A common and immediate response justifies and glorifies this message; such as, "The other day I went to a fight and a hockey game broke out". This appears to be the mindset which justifies inappropriate expressions of anger. There is a fundamental problem with this mindset; it does not create awareness of accountability and consequences.

"The other day I went to a fight and a hockey game broke out."

Take some time to consider the following questions. Reflect on where you learned your anger style(s) and how they affect you today.

1. What adults taught you about your type of anger and how?

_____

_____

_____

2. What does your type of anger do to you?

_____

_____

_____

3. What does your type of anger do to others?

_____

_____

_____

Drama Triangle

The drama triangle is a common way anger is expressed. It is based on right versus wrong, black or white thinking. The characters in the following drama triangle are the Persecutor, the Victim and the Rescuer.[11] These are all roles we take on at different times, depending on the situation. The roles can, and do, shift. They can be an internal struggle or acted out with others. Because we repress our feelings, we are usually unaware of the roles we play. The drama of the triangle is created by the pain of our wounds and fueled by our expectations (Table 7).

---

[11] "Fairy Tales and Script Drama Analysis," Stephen S. Karpman, M.D., Transactional Analysis Bulletin, 1968.

Table 7
The Drama Triangle

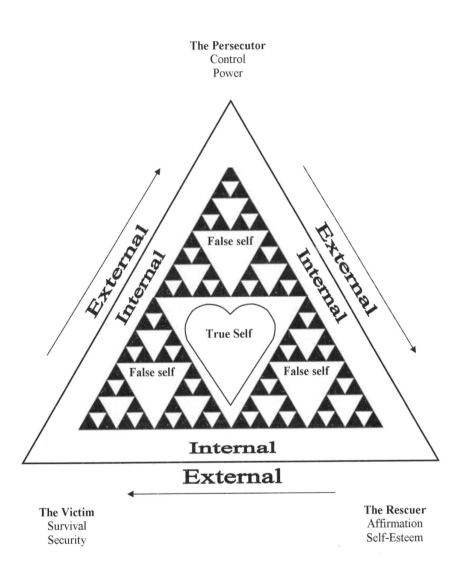

The common thread of each role is **MANIPULATION.**

Harry's Example of the Drama Triangle

One morning, I was looking forward to taking my usual glass of orange juice with my pills when I discovered that my teenage daughter had taken the last of the juice. I became incensed, and sharply criticized her for being selfish and inconsiderate. My wife overheard my harsh words and quickly interceded to defend our daughter, who was hurt by my shaming tone of voice. My wife, feeling the need to protect our daughter, became the **Rescuer**. Our daughter, who had been chastised, was the **Victim**. I, in my judgments, was the **Persecutor**. My wife then turned and chastised me for my critical tone; I felt guilty and hurt. Our daughter apologized for taking the last of the juice to help me feel better. My wife had become the **Persecutor**. I was the new **Victim**. Our daughter was now the **Rescuer**.

THE COMMON THREAD OF EACH ROLE IS MANIPULATION.

This revolving drama triangle plays out in our families, at work, and in our relationships. It creates an unhealthy way of connecting and prevents us from resolving differences, ultimately pushing us to avoid intimacy.

Remember, the drama triangle is based upon right versus wrong thinking. The Persecutor is "right" in his or her judgment. The Victim is "right" in feeling wronged. The Rescuer is "right" in determining that the Victim needs help.

The drama triangle is one way repression is repeated daily in our lives. The common thread of each role is manipulation. We may consciously or unconsciously, in each role we play, try to get the other person to do what we feel we want. Manipulation also is often experienced internally between our true self and false self. We experience external drama resulting from the unresolved internal drama between our true self and our false self. Our beliefs about who we are were fostered by the drama triangles of our childhood. Knowing who I am, my true self, frees me from proving who I am.

Each of these roles is an outgrowth of our false self. The false self is seeking control and power as the persecutor, survival and security as the victim, and affirmation and self-esteem as the rescuer.

Reflecting back on Harry's story, his false self felt hurt and rejected by his daughter's action. Feeling wounded, Harry's false self desired to control the situation. When his wife rescued their daughter by confronting him, his false self felt his security threatened. When his daughter apologized, his false self felt affirmed.

Internal and external drama triangles are difficult to detect. Understanding the process will help you avoid unnecessary pain. When have you found yourself in a drama triangle? Think about a time when you played each of the leading roles (Table 7). Chances are good that it has occurred in the last twenty-four hours. Then, using Table 8, complete the answer for each question.

> KNOWING WHO I AM, MY TRUE SELF, FREES ME FROM PROVING WHO I AM.

Table 8
Discovering Your Roles in the Drama Triangles

Reflect on and answer the following questions:

1. When and how was I victimized as a child?

2. When and how was I a rescuer as a child?

3. When and how was I a persecutor as a child?

4. When and how was I victimized as an adult?

5. When and how was I a rescuer as an adult?

6. When and how was I a persecutor as an adult?

You have in all likelihood received much new information, so don't feel pressured to move quickly, especially with the exercises in the book, now and later.

Twenty-One Lessons (Table 9) is a summary of significant points to remember and to continue to use as a foundation for the remaining chapters.

Table 9
Twenty-one Lessons Learned About Anger

1. Everyone has anger.

2. Anger is an emotion.

3. Emotions, like colors, are not right or wrong.

4. Emotions need to be validated not obeyed.

5. Anger is the guardian of our self-esteem.

6. I am not my anger.

7. Everyone uses repression.

8. Repression can be hurtful or helpful.

9. What we don't know can hurt ourselves and others.

10. Repression causes our blind spots.

11. Repression is responsible for the creation of our false self.

12. The mask of defensiveness that we wear is our false self.

13. The cost of our masks is the loss of intimacy with us and others.

14. Removing our masks reveals our true selves.

15. Our true self is a 10.

16. There are two types and ten styles of anger.

17. Implosive anger is as destructive as explosive anger.

18. My feeling of anger and my angry behavior are separate.

19. My anger styles were modeled for me.

20. Anger is either LOVE-BASED or FEAR-BASED.

21. Anger is a GIFT.

CHAPTER 3

THE LAW OF SUPER-SATURATION:

"I've had it! Something's got to give."

Regina is masterful at juggling the demands of a very busy family. Getting three children to school, to various athletic and music practices and keeping up the house are beginning to wear on her. The kids are doing so well though and Larry's work is so demanding. No wonder he is gone so much and does little around the house. She hasn't had lunch with her friends in four weeks though. And hasn't read a book or even the newspaper in who knows how long.

She notices sleep is not as restful and her temper has flared in ways that surprise her. She wonders if this is what being super-saturated means.

What is super-saturation? More importantly, how or why does it matter? Technically, super-saturation means to increase the concentration of a chemical beyond a solution's ability to keep the chemical in liquid form. For our purposes, this means filling up beyond capacity. Certain chemicals will crystallize when they exceed their saturation point; the chemicals will change abruptly to a new form. Humans are subject to this "crystallization" effect through super-saturation when they blow up or withdraw.

Super-saturation is like wiping up a water spill with a sponge that is already full. It is attempting to pour water into a glass that is already full. We become emotionally super-saturated when we try without success to be nice or do too much, thereby unknowingly repressing emotions. This is living like a glass filled to the brim with irritation, frustration, cynicism, resentment and bitterness.

HUMANS ARE SUBJECT TO THIS "CRYSTALLIZATION" EFFECT THROUGH SUPER-SATURATION

Super-saturation can go two ways, outward or inward. Surprisingly, many who would describe themselves as empty, sad or void of anger are sitting on a buried fuse. A sudden or trivial event will provoke an unexpected outburst which is out of proportion to the event. It's simply over the top. On the other hand, a lack of outward response may cause anger to saturate inwardly where it does an unrecognized slow burn, becoming the twin sister of anger: sadness. This can be experienced as numbness, despair, gloom, pessimism, depression, high blood pressure, headaches and other physical symptoms resulting from intellectualized anger.

Anger from inward or outward super-saturation requires an intense amount of energy. Its eruption, however, leads to harming of others or self. Self-directed anger leads to a process of shutting down and closing off. Other-directed anger leads to bruised or broken relationships. Both of these types of anger expression can happen suddenly and are unnecessary.

We have all heard of extreme cases of human super-saturation crystallizing into violence: the man who became so irate with the IRS that he flew a plane into their building, killing himself and others or the gunmen who shot innocent people in the school or fast food restaurant.

There are less extreme examples of anger from super-saturation that occur every day in our homes, stores, businesses and on our highways. It is seen in our relationships with friends and loved ones, even strangers. Anger is visible through our responses of sarcasm and cynicism. The anger is often subtle, such as not returning a phone call or not following through on a task. Maybe it's yelling at the kids for not picking up their toys or leaving their bikes in the driveway. It could be not leaving on time for a lunch appointment or being late for work. Super-saturation is commonly seen when we interrupt someone else who is talking or just tune them out. It could be a channel surfer that frustrates everyone else in the room. Let's not forget road rage and the gestures some people use when driving.

Maybe you have experienced the robotic, micro-manager looking at his or her watch as you walk into work. Don't forget the co-worker who is constantly making everything a competition. At some companies, your good is never good enough or you are expected to work more hours for less pay. Others go to work dreaming about their ideal employment but feel stuck day after day of going nowhere. You may feel unappreciated or disrespected at work or home. You may be married to someone who nags or has unrealistic expectations. You may find yourself constantly arguing over the smallest issues with your significant other. Maybe the children exceed their cell phone minutes or texts. How many cell phones have you purchased for the kids? Don't answer that question or you might super-saturate just thinking about it!

The Physiology of Anger: Adrenaline, Oxytocin, and Our Reaction to Super-Saturation

Jim comes home stressed to the max by the continuing frustrations at work. He is irritable and on edge.

"Did you get the dry cleaning?" Connie asks as he walks in the door.

Jim explodes, "What do you mean, 'did I get the dry cleaning?' What do you expect after the day I've had?!"Defensively she says, "I was only wondering ..."

Jim cuts her off in midsentence, his anger increasing. "Don't you even care what my day was like? You seem to have no idea what I have to put up with."

"Listen, I've had a bad day too," she retorts.

"That does it!" he yells as his anger escalates, moving closer, now in her face. "You are an uncaring, selfish woman!"

Jim backs her up against the kitchen wall. As she cowers, Jan becomes increasingly anxious about where his anger is going yet again. Almost immediately, her thoughts go to the children upstairs and what they are hearing or what they are feeling. Just as quickly, Jim notices the subtle, but definite, change in her eyes and her shift in attention. His anger escalates further and with the veins in his neck popping out, he screams, "Look at me!"

Similar confrontations are happening with significant frequency. Most are less intense, but some are even more so. These disagreements are occurring not just in marriages but also at work, on the interstate, at the checkout counter and on the phone. Such interactions are mediated by the stress hormone adrenaline. Understanding the role of adrenaline lets us craft a response to provocation that decreases the potential for damage to others and to ourselves.

The scenario above shows the effects of hormones on anger, adrenaline and, recently recognized, oxytocin.

Adrenaline is well recognized for the effect called the "fight or flight reaction." This reaction is a rapid, biological mechanism. For primitive man, this instinct evolved as a protective mechanism when confronted with a frightening threat to his life. This biological reaction almost instantly increased his chance for survival by improving stamina, sharpening focus on the threat, and greatly increasing tolerance for pain. These effects prepared him for a successful "fight" with the threat or for escaping the threat by a "flight" to safety. Once the physical energy to fight or flee was expended, adrenaline levels quickly returned to normal.

It is crucial to know that the likelihood for a fight or flight reaction in today's world does not come from a physical threat. The most common threat today is from an emotional/psychological source. This threat is to our self-esteem or our self-worth. We will explore this area of emotional/psychological vulnerability a few pages later. For our current purpose, we emphasize the extremely rapid onset and strength to which this reaction can build. Most of us have been victims of and witnessed this reactivity.

There can be useful benefits for the reaction. These benefits come to us in emergencies, such as a house fire or a car wreck. The same benefits occur in active sports such as football, baseball and soccer. Adrenaline gives the person or the athlete greater stamina, an increased ability to focus on the immediate surroundings, and a greatly increased tolerance for pain. However, reactivity from unnecessary defensiveness leads to negative results. What we see in the "real" world is the potential for hurt and pain resulting from an increase of adrenaline, caused by the threat to our self-esteem. Super-saturation decreases our tolerance to such challenges.

Men/Women: Similarities and Differences

Adrenaline is usually thought of as a "male" hormone since men seem to be more often engulfed by its effect. Jim's story demonstrates this theory.

The more recently discovered hormone oxytocin seems to be more of a "female" hormone. Among its effects are the ability to decrease blood pressure, pulse and even cholesterol. Other research suggests oxytocin prompts our desire for community, and is known as a "buffer" for the impact of adrenaline. By itself, oxytocin encourages a "tend and befriend" reaction; "tend" to the nest (home, children) and "befriend" others. Connie demonstrates the effects of adrenaline with her brief outward retort, "Listen, I've had a bad day, too." Oxytocin's effect quickly follows by buffering the adrenaline she experiences, thereby allowing her attention to shift to concern about the children.

Significant research in the Harvard Nurses' Health Study highlights the effect of befriending.[12] Over the course of nine years, the nurses with more friends had noticeably fewer health related problems associated with aging. In addition, after the nine years, they had 60% less chance of dying prematurely.

---

[12] "UCLA Study on Friendship among Women," by Gale Berkowitz, 2007, www.thelifemanagementalliance.com

Other research suggests that even for men, oxytocin prompts a desire for community.

In the scenario above, Connie shows an example of the "tend" reaction. Her attention quickly turns to concern for the children. In the same example, Jim's hyper-focus on his wife from adrenaline instantly senses her shifting attention, which escalates his anger.

Expectations about Anger for Men and Women

Society seems to say that a man's anger is ok while a woman's is not. In sports, home, work and of course political discussions, a man's anger is tolerated and, to some extent, expected. Yet, a woman's display of assertiveness or aggression is commonly judged as unacceptable.

> A WOMAN'S DISPLAY OF ASSERTIVENESS IS COMMONLY JUDGED AS UNACCEPTABLE.

The more common pattern in a serious marital disagreement is for the husband to exert control. First, he may make an effort to restore things to where they were. Failing that attempt, he may become rejecting, cold and perhaps even threatening to end the relationship.

His message will generally say, "You are wrong and I can show you why. Change back and I will accept you again. If you don't, there will be consequences."

What most women seem to learn in a protracted, disagreeable relationship is silent submission, ineffective fighting, blaming and emotional distancing. In effect, she denies herself. Her efforts to minimize conflict by showing or pretending closeness do not equal intimacy. Over time, the anger will turn to bitterness, avoidance and even thoughts of revenge.

The hormones adrenaline and oxytocin, societal expectations, and our life experience combine to influence the way our anger is expressed. In general, men express their anger outward by using harsh words or yelling; women tend to go inward which contributes to their higher incidence of sadness and depression. At the same time, many men internalize their anger and many women become explosive.

Being full to the brim with anger, hurt, shame or sadness becomes the breeding ground for an explosion or implosion of unhealthy anger.

How Do We Super-Saturate?

Super-saturating occurs when we do not make time for ourselves to empty our glass. We are too busy and, therefore, become out of balance. One scenario might be taking care of a parent who is constantly complaining and wanting you to make them happy. Perhaps it is poor money management, running in the rat race of robbing Peter to pay Paul.

The evidence of super-saturation has many forms. You may find ways to numb out through alcohol, drugs, affairs, porn, sports, television, online games, work, gambling, eating, or shopping. Maybe you find yourself verbally abusing others. You may even hit a spouse or family member in a moment of anger.

It doesn't take much to become overly saturated. Often it's a slow burn that bursts into an obvious fire, creating pain and suffering. The words of regret quickly follow: "I'm so sorry. I didn't mean that. It just came out of nowhere." Well, not really! The feelings do come from somewhere. These responses are the result of super-saturation. We are human and will experience saturation repeatedly. Some results will be more severe than others, yet there is a cost at any level.

We lose a part of ourselves each time we are out of balance. Remember the definition of super-saturation is to saturate abnormally or beyond our limits. It is unhealthy to lose a part of ourselves. It is also unhealthy to deny that every choice has a consequence, every action has a reaction.

It is common to forget the times we have hurt others or ourselves. It is also common to justify our behaviors. We create a false persona that all is well and that our actions really didn't hurt anyone. Unfortunately, such a mask only fools us. Words and actions leave wounds and scars; some have healed and some remain open...

At some point, super-saturation can be used to our advantage. Super-saturation tells us, "I've had it and something's got to give." Taking healthy action is for the courageous! It's for those who say, "Enough is enough! I am sick and tired of being sick and tired. I want out and I want healthy! I want to heal the wounds I have experienced and caused." Super-saturation becomes our ally at this point. Although it will not reverse the past damage, it will create a platform for establishing new beliefs and new behaviors that promote healing.

How Stress Contributes to Super-Saturation

We understand stress to be the amount and intensity of change in our lives, as described by Miller and Rahe.[13] They point out that severe stress occurs with such life events as the death of a spouse or a divorce. Less severe, and yet still noticeable, is stress that follows from receiving a traffic ticket or even going on a vacation. Their study has confirmed that a high stress score is correlated with an increased rate of illness.

---

[13] Miller, M and Rahe, R.H. *Life Changes Scaling for the 1990s.* Journal of Psychosomatic Research, 43:279-292,1997

Use the Miller-Rahe Stress Scale (Table 10) to evaluate your recent stress level. Read through the list of life events and check each one that applies to you. There is no right or wrong score. Each person's score is like a dipstick that measures the level of oil in your car. Your score can alert you to areas in your life that need attention in order to decrease the negative effects of accumulated stress.

Table 10
Miller and Rahe Stress Scale

Work through Miller and Rahe's list of life events. Score your "life change units" for events you have experienced in the last year. Afterwards, total your score.

Life Event	Life Change Units	Your Score
Major change in health or behavior of family member	55	
Marriage	50	
Pregnancy	67	
Miscarriage or abortion	65	
Gain of a new family member:		
Birth of a child	66	
Adoption of a child	65	
A relative moving in with you	59	
Spouse beginning or ending work	46	
Child leaving home:		
To attend college	41	
Due to marriage	41	
For other reasons	45	
Change in arguments with spouse	50	
In-law problems	38	
Change in marital status of parents:		
Divorce	59	
Remarriage	50	
Separation from spouse:		
Due to work	53	
Due to marital problems	76	
Divorce	96	
Birth of grandchild	43	
Death of spouse	119	
Death of other family member:		
Child	123	
Brother or sister	102	
Parent	100	

Personal and social:		
Change in personal habits	26	
Beginning or ending school or college	38	
Change of school or college	35	
Change in political beliefs	24	
Change in religious beliefs	29	
Change in social activity	27	
Vacation	24	
New, close, personal relationship	37	
Engagement to marry	45	
Girlfriend of boyfriend problems	39	
Sexual difficulties	44	
"Falling out" of close personal relationship	47	
An accident	48	
Minor violation of the law	20	
Being held in jail	75	
Death of a close friend	70	
Major decision regarding your immediate future	51	
Major personal achievement	36	
Financial:		
Major change in finances		
Increased income	38	
Decreased income	60	
Investment and/or credit difficulties	56	
Lost or damaged personal property	43	
Moderate purchase	20	
Major purchase	37	
Foreclosure or mortgage or loan	58	
Total		

Score of 450+: Worrisome
Score of 301-450: Fair
Score of 150-300: Good
Score 150-: Excellent

CHAPTER 4

❤

THE LAW OF CONFESSION:
"Wow, I really do have blind spots."

*T*he first three chapters have been an exploration into the less obvious elements of fear-based anger. In the first and second chapters, the concept of blind spots was introduced and its powerful effect on the internal aspects of anger. These blind spots can be compared to kindling used to start a campfire. The third chapter introduced super-saturation that has the effect of introducing a match to the kindling. Acknowledging repression and super-saturation leads to the fourth law, the "Law of Confession."

Jim, 44, has been married to Denise for 18 years. They have two children, with the youngest is about to graduate high school. For several years, Jim has worked successfully as a manufacturer's rep. His commitment and attention to detail have played a major role in his success. However, his wife has complained about his perfectionism and his distance from her for several years. In fact, she files for divorce four months ago despite numerous visits to a marriage counselor. She told him she felt controlled even smothered by him, and didn't see him changing at all.

Jim sought help for himself to find out "what do I need to do to save my marriage?" With the counselor's feedback, he began to see that his behavior was offensive to her. It even became clear that trying to please her was offensive.

This recognition brought a welcome sense of relief and a desire to make changes in his way of relating to her. He knew that a first step was to "confess", that is to acknowledge to her how hurtful his behavior had been. He was surprised to see the slight thawing of her resistance to him. He knows there was much for him to change.

A dictionary[14] tells us that to confess means to acknowledge or admit incompetence or wrongdoing. Confessing needs to include the acknowledgement of wrongdoing we have done to ourselves, and that we have done to others. Repression keeps much of the pain we received and we gave out of our awareness. This repression was a survival tool for us. As adults, however, we no longer need to just survive. Confessing is a step toward thriving.

The following exercise (Table 11) is designed to help you recognize and possibly re-experience the anger you have received and given. Follow the instructions and allow your feelings to resurface. As you undertake this exercise, turn to moments when you received anger and when you gave it. Bring to mind the memories: images, voices, feelings. Then, think of ten instances in which you received anger and ten instances when you gave anger. Write from the point of view of your age and context in which you lived at the time. Be brief but thorough enough to convey the impact of each experience. Table 12

---

[14] Webster's Dictionary

will give you some ideas of people in your life that might fit this exercise.

As an example, Harry shares an instance from his life concerning his father. You can use Harry's examples to think of people in your own life.

Harry's Life Example
Anger Received

What did your father do or say? At about age ten, I was sitting at a high work bench in the basement building a model airplane. I was completely engrossed in what was pretty intricate work. I sensed my father coming and waited with feelings of dread. Sure enough, he came beside me and said, "Let me help you." I felt apprehension, even fear about what might happen. His offer of help was really a command. Within moments, he pushed me off the stool and broke the airplane I was working on.

What did it do to you? I felt helpless, powerless and rejected. I felt humiliated and then quickly became furious.

Anger Given

What did you do or say? After my father broke the airplane in the description above, I ran to the basement door and, out of fear and anger, turned to him, and with venom in my voice shouted, "Why do you always have to ruin everything?" After I yelled at him, I felt a shift in my feelings, as if to say, "You won't hurt me anymore!"

What did it do to him? After I yelled at him, his head seemed to sink over the workbench. The situation was never again referred to after I left the room. In hindsight, I believe he felt wounded and ashamed.

What did you lose because of this anger? I lost trust in my father. I became afraid of receiving anger from anyone. I became emotionally isolated and wouldn't talk about my feelings. This fear of anger caused me to have problems with closeness in all my relationships, well into my 40s.

Table 11
Anger Received and Given

○ *Find a quiet place where you can be alone. Begin thinking about your life following the directions below.*

○ *Think about one person in your life with whom you have received and given anger. In the form below, answer the questions about this person's interaction with you.*

○ *Then, think about* **at least, but not limited to, 10** *instances of receiving and giving anger involving significant people in your life. Browse through the sample list of people and issues in Table 12 to help you identify those relationships, or create your own.*

○ *Be specific. Be clear. Be honest.*

○ *If more space is needed, feel free to use an extra sheet.*

○ *Remember, you will only get out of this what you put into it.*

Write Name of Person/Issue _____

Anger Received

What did this person do or say? Anger you received as a child, teenager or adult:

_____

_____

_____

What did it do to you?

_____

_____

_____

Anger Given

What did you do or say? Anger you gave to this person:

_____

_____

_____

What did it do to him/her?

_____

_____

_____

What did you lose because of this anger?

_____

_____

_____

How does this affect you today?

_____

_____

_____

Table 12
List of Choices of Anger Received/Given

Father	Step-Father	Mother
Step-Mother	Grandfather	Grandmother
Foster Parent	Guardian	Spouse/Partner
Ex-Spouse/Partner	Ex-Boyfriend/ Girlfriend/ Fiancé	Father/Mother of your child
Your child/children	Step-child/children	Sibling(s)
Boss	Co-worker	Teacher
Classmate	Friend	Don't know who they are
Other relationship	Pornography	Abuse (sexual/emotional/ mental/verbal)
Alcohol	Drugs	God

The anger received and anger given exercise is effective in realizing past pain, defenses, and blind spots. These realizations will move you toward healing your relationships with yourself and others.

Confession includes four steps:

1. Verbalizing the inappropriate action.
2. Empathizing with the other person's pain caused by that action.
3. Accepting sole responsibility for our actions.
4. Asking for forgiveness in an appropriate manner and without expectation.

Verbalizing the Inappropriate Action

You may have noticed that writing out instances of anger, received and given, allows for feelings and thoughts to be processed together. It takes the free floating energy of the past into the present for healing. No running or denial, the proof is right there in front of you. Evaluate the situations by documenting: "This is what happened. This is what it did to me. This is what it did to others. This is how it affects me today."

Now review what you have written and ask, "How honest have I been? How thorough have I been?" It is normal to feel stuck here; denial runs deep. Sometimes, it takes experiential exercises and coaching to get to the heart of our pain. It would be easy to avoid these experiences or rationalize them away. However, the heart of someone who is courageous will not let this happen.

LOVE-BASED ANGER SAYS, "I WILL LEARN NEW WAYS TO DEAL WITH PAST, PRESENT AND FUTURE INAPPROPRIATE ACTIONS."

Damage done in the heart cannot be healed with mere words alone. Love-based anger says, "I will learn new ways to deal with past, present and future inappropriate actions." Since none of us are perfect, we can take the opportunity to fail forward. The first step is to acknowledge the inappropriate action associated with our anger. It is even better to journal these actions to help you see the bigger picture. We would encourage you to find an accountability partner who will help you process what happened and add another perspective.

For most of us, our anger is connected to assumptions and expectations. When these expectations are not met, it is natural to become angry or disappointed. As you review each occurrence on your worksheets, look for the underlying expectation. Once you are clear with what took place, you will be in a place where you can verbalize what happened.

Let's say that you asked your spouse to mail a package while you were out of town. When you came home, the first thing you noticed was the package still on the counter. Your first response might be to share your frustration and disappointment with a comment that goes something like this: "Are you kidding? What's wrong with you? I needed this package sent out while I was gone and you agreed to do it. Can't you do anything right?" Now, some of you might be saying, "What's wrong with that? Makes sense to me." We hope to be seeing you at the workshop soon. Just kidding! Obviously, this approach was inappropriate and over the top.

FOR MOST OF US, OUR ANGER IS CONNECTED TO ASSUMPTIONS AND EXPECTATIONS.

There are typically truths as well as lies in our actions and words. In this case, the truth was the disappointment and frustration you might have felt over your spouse's lack of follow-through. There is nothing wrong with being disappointed or frustrated; that is a natural response. The lie is that there is something wrong with the person because of their behavior. When a person asks, "What's wrong with you? Can't you do anything right?" the words are disrespectful judgments and simply inappropriate.

These situations go awry when we allow our frustrations, disappointments and anger to convince us we are right. If I am right, then someone must be wrong. My inappropriate actions and words are not justified because my expectations were not met. In this illustration, you might journal this event as follows: I asked my spouse to mail a package while I was gone. When I got home, it was still on the counter which really frustrated me. This package needed to be at a certain place at a certain time to accomplish a deadline. Now, I look like a failure because of my spouse's lack of follow-through. What I said was, "Are you kidding? What's wrong with you? I needed this package sent out while I was gone and you agreed to do it. Can't you do anything right?"

Think about your response. What did this situation do to you? Did you feel like a failure? Did you feel the need to blame to protect yourself?

Now, think about the spouse in this situation. What did this conflict do to the other person? Did it make them feel insignificant, as if they can't do anything right?

What are the truths in this scenario? The spouse was asked to mail something. The urgency of the package needing to be mailed was not conveyed. The responsibility for something important was shifted to someone else. A judgment was made about the spouse's lack of follow-through. Failure was felt because the package didn't arrive on time.

What are the truths about the spouse? He or she did not mail the package. There is no information about why the package was not mailed.

IT TAKES CONSCIOUS EFFORT AND WILLINGNESS TO FEEL YOUR FEELINGS WITHOUT COMMUNICATING INAPPROPRIATE WORDS OR BEHAVIORS.

How are both of you affected today? There will be frustration, mistrust, distancing, and potential paybacks. This one event will affect communication and intimacy.

The progression of this story leads to a dead end or a blind canyon. Both now feel justified in their judgments. The situation becomes a stalemate. Does this scenario seem familiar? Have you been in this place? This example is the heart of the drama triangle.

UNTIL YOU IDENTIFY AND BEGIN TO HEAL YOUR OWN PAIN, FEAR, HURT AND SHAME, YOUR ACTIONS WILL APPEAR INSINCERE.

It takes a courageous heart to move past a stalemate, especially one filled with hurt and anger. The courageous approach looks, sounds, and *is* different. It is a conscious decision to be real and honest about your feelings, while having the other person's benefit in mind.

Verbalizing in an appropriate manner would sound more like this "Honey, it was inappropriate of me to suggest there is something wrong with you and to say you can't do anything right. I had no right to talk to you that way and I regret the way I treated you." It takes conscious effort and willingness to feel your feelings without communicating inappropriate words or behaviors.

This example also assumes that the couple is committed to a healthy way of relating.

It would be nice if we had a handy manual to pull out when we needed the right thing to say. However, it takes more than a manual. Conscious effort and willingness to realize your feelings without projecting inappropriate words or behaviors are the keys to success. Our previously learned responses have become well-ingrained, taking on the characteristics of muscle memory. Changing those responses and communicating effectively takes training, practice, and persistence. We have been practicing the old behaviors for years and it is unrealistic to expect a quick change for the better. Practice does not make perfect; practice makes permanent! We have a choice in what we choose to practice.

REMORSE IS THE BEGINNING STEP TOWARD HEALING YOURSELF AND EMPATHIZING WITH THE ONES WHO'VE BEEN HURT.

Empathizing with the Other Person's Pain

Confession is not complete without empathy. Empathy, from the Greek root word meaning "feeling," is the action of understanding, being aware of and sensitive to the feelings and thoughts of another. It is the meta-message that confirms that our confession is sincere. A flippant, non-emotional apology conveys the message of insincerity. We all know that a tone of voice and facial expressions are ultimately more significant than the actual words themselves. We cannot heal the damage done by our actions with words alone. Just as they were in causing pain, our actions must be a part of the healing process.

An insincere confession engenders more distrust on the part of the offended. It encourages a continual cycle of defensiveness, hurt and distancing. In an insincere confession, the offender has not identified the pain which prompted the aggressive, painful action toward the other person. Until you identify and begin to heal your own pain, fear, hurt and shame, your actions will appear insincere. Forgiving yourself gives you the freedom to forgive the other person and to identify with their feelings. Insincere confessions keep us captive to our previous experiences, keeping us trapped in the prison of the familiar. Remorse is the beginning step toward healing yourself and empathizing with the ones who've been hurt.

BLAMING SOMEONE ELSE, IS "LEARNED HELPLESSNESS."

The bad news is that we are the problem; the better news is that we are the problem but have the power to become our own agents of change. We are what we know until we choose to change. It's not who we are, it's what we have learned. We can only change ourselves.

It is difficult to empathize with another's pain until we have identified with our own pain. Identifying our own pain allows us to sincerely connect with the pain we may have caused. The courageous heart is willing to walk in the shoes of another person and convey with words, tones and action a desire to repair the damage done by an offense.

Accepting Sole Responsibility for our Actions

A sincere effort to repair the relationship must include the offender's willingness to accept sole responsibility for their hurtful actions and their consequences. Another person's words or behavior do not excuse our choice to cause pain. Even though the other person may behave in a hurtful way, the courageous heart attempts to break the defensive cycle by accepting sole responsibility for its behavior.

Excusing behavior by blaming someone else, or claiming we can't help ourselves when angry, is learned helplessness. The responsibility of our behavior is ours and ours alone, no matter how much we protest or justify.

By taking to heart this responsibility, we are on the path of the courageous. The path may be difficult, even painful, as we change old, familiar beliefs and behaviors. Yet, the price of change is worth more than we can anticipate, bringing peace of mind, clarity about who we are and new found confidence.

Confession alone does not undo damage. A sincere confession involves letting go of how the offended party will respond. Any confession that includes words of explanation or justification often invalidates the confession.

Confession may cause a laundry list of possible outcomes from mild to severe: a cold shoulder, harsh words, the silent treatment, sleeping in different beds, protracted distancing, loss of intimacy, separation, financial loss, divorce, and possible imprisonment. It takes courage to accept that we are not in control of the outcome of our confession.

> A SINCERE CONFESSION INVOLVES LETTING GO OF HOW THE OFFENDED PARTY WILL RESPOND.

Asking for Forgiveness in an Appropriate Manner

A confession is not complete without eventually asking for forgiveness in an appropriate manner. A confession will not be sincere without humility. The courageous heart is humble and chooses to submit; we give up the "right" to control the outcome. Caring about the relationship means being more concerned about the process, the way we do something, rather than the goal.

Summary

Confession begins with restating the offense such as, "I know I hurt you when I used a sarcastic tone of voice. It was inappropriate and unnecessary." It proceeds by empathizing with the pain we caused and acknowledging responsibility such as saying, "I am sorry for what I did." A complete confession concludes with a humble question: "Will you forgive me"? Simply going through the motions of the apology without heartfelt intention is manipulation. This process most likely will feel awkward and uncomfortable in the beginning because it takes us out of our comfort zone and old familiar words.

CHAPTER 5

THE LAW OF RECONCILIATION:

"Okay, I'm ready to be honest and start changing."

Reconciliation has been variously defined as: to make amends, set things right, smooth rough edges, amend mistreatment of others, connect up again, make up, get back together, re-establish relationships and create unity from diversity.

Reconciliation begins with one's self, a concept that some may find revolutionary or unacceptable. It follows the principle of, "Love your neighbor as yourself." Loving one's self is the basis for loving others. Therefore, reconciliation has to begin with ourselves. Making amends involves an understanding of how our emotions, intellect and will are intimately connected.

We are more than our emotions or intellect. Our emotions can masquerade as guideposts for decision making; yet, they are primarily based upon impressions rather than facts. Our experiences influence our emotional sense of what is right or wrong. We are not referring to moral absolutes of right or wrong but rather to our personal choices and preferences.

As a result of our upbringing and experiences, we will develop beliefs that influence our use of emotional and intellectual skills. A significant percentage of our beliefs are subconscious, yet directly affect our use of our emotions and intellect. These unrecognized beliefs are blind spots and become the basis for the reconciliation with self.

Because of these blind spots we tend to develop ways of reacting that have become ingrained to the point of muscle memory. Our defenses have been developed to protect our wounded hearts. Our blind spots hide these necessary defenses from our awareness, causing us to repeatedly behave in ways we regret. Reconciliation involves healing the wounded heart, developing congruent beliefs, and receiving love and forgiveness from self and others.

RECONCILIATION INVOLVES HEALING THE WOUNDED HEART...

We can move past reacting to a menu of responses. Responding requires the discipline of placing our intellect in charge of our decisions rather than giving power to our feelings. The following formula provides a foundation for understanding the difference between feelings of anger and actions resulting from anger. The table illustrates the difference between reacting and responding.

R^1=Responding R^2=Reacting

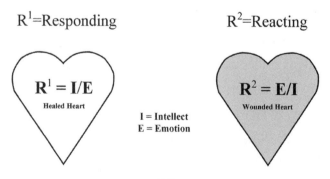

$$R^1 = I/E$$
Healed Heart

$$R^2 = E/I$$
Wounded Heart

I = Intellect
E = Emotion

In this formula, "R^1" (on the left) represents responding, "I" refers to intellect and "E" is emotions, surrounded by a healthy heart. By comparison, reacting (on the right) is represented by $R^2=E/I$, surrounded by the wounded heart.

The condition of our heart is critical to our ability to develop more effective ways of responding. Healing the damage done to the heart begins with intellectual awareness; we cannot heal or change what we don't first acknowledge. Then, we must move the damage through our feelings to a place that allows healing of the heart. "You cannot get through it, until you go through it, until it goes through you." Remember, damage done to the heart cannot be healed with the head.

> "YOU CANNOT GET THROUGH IT, UNTIL YOU GO THROUGH IT, UNTIL IT GOES THROUGH YOU."

The *Heart of the Courageous* experiential seminar is a journey from the head to the heart. The workshop begins with validating emotions and clarifying their impact on beliefs and behaviors. Emotions, while valid, have often been given false meaning. Although my anger may be valid, it does not justify an inappropriate action, such as raising my voice, turning my back on my partner in bed, or steaming on the inside while biting my tongue.

The "ABCs of Emotions" is an acronym to help understand responding versus reacting. The ABCs are "adversity, belief, and consequence," as described by Marcia Powers.[15]

---

[15] Powers, Marcia, *The Dragon Slayer With a Heavy Heart: A Powerful Story About Finding Happiness and Serenity...Even When You Really, Really Wish Some Things Were Different* , (Wilshire Book Co. 2003) p. 58.

A dversity: Something happens

B elief: Views, thoughts about what happened

C onsequences: Resulting feelings and actions

Adversity is a condition marked by misfortune, calamity, and distress. We all know that adversity is a given in life and no one is immune. Eventually, each one of us will face hardship where we have the option to react or respond. When something hard happens, we either get bitter or get better. Our attitude towards misfortune is a choice. Adversities will happen.

EVENTUALLY, EACH ONE OF US WILL FACE HARDSHIP WHERE WE HAVE THE OPTION TO REACT OR RESPOND.

Beliefs are opinions, convictions or creeds. They are the eye glasses through which we see and interpret ourselves, others, and the world. Our beliefs determine what we think. If I believe I am unworthy, my thoughts will confirm that belief. Beliefs may be true or false; regardless, they influence our decisions and behaviors.

Consequences are the results of the influence our subjective beliefs have on the adverse event. We will make a decision based upon the feelings that arise from our beliefs. For example, if my belief system says that the accent in your voice tells me you are from a culture that is a threat to me, I will make one decision about what to do. On the other hand, if your accent is pleasing to me, I will most likely make a different decision.

These ABCs clarify that the consequences, feelings and actions, in response to an adversity, are determined by our beliefs, views and thoughts about what happened. In other words, what we feel and do is determined by our beliefs.

A common misunderstanding is that feelings determine beliefs. If it feels right it must be right. Conversely, if it doesn't feel right it must be wrong.

In fact, the opposite is true. The reality is our beliefs are in charge, not feelings. When I change my beliefs I can more readily create a favorable outcome, regardless of my feelings. I am not my feelings. Doing the right thing will usually feel uncomfortable when it goes counter to an old belief.

For example, when an argument begins a common reaction is to feel threatened and become defensive. My old beliefs may tell me I am threatened. However, when I use the "pause" button for my reacting, I have the opportunity to examine the real circumstance. I might then conclude that I am not in actual danger. This is what can be called an "emotional coat check",

...WHAT WE FEEL AND DO IS DETERMINED BY OUR BELIEFS.

that is, choosing to set emotions aside and think. It is as if I have taken the position of a disinterested bystander. I can now look at the facts of this threat rather than have my defensive feelings decide for me.

The emotional coat check is like checking my coat at the theater. I put my emotions aside for the moment to objectively examine my beliefs. My belief system defines what I perceive. In turn, what I perceive defines what is real for me. My current belief system becomes the window through which the world is perceived. Prior experiences shape and define belief systems and, therefore, behaviors. These experiences are often emotionally charged and hinder the ability to objectively examine the current situation.

Emotions are neither right nor wrong. However, most of us have been taught that there is a right or wrong answer to anger. When anger occurs, we must believe we are either right or wrong and we will act accordingly. This belief is the same as saying: "I and my anger are one." By employing the emotional coat check, we allow ourselves to see that we are not our anger. If I am not my anger, then I have the freedom to choose what I say or do. The ability to choose my response establishes a new belief system. We are free from the previous crooked and distorted beliefs. Our experiences may have shaped us, but they do not define us. We are more than our experiences.

OUR EXPERIENCES MAY HAVE SHAPED US, BUT THEY DO NOT DEFINE US.

Turning the Coals of the Past into the Diamonds of the Present

Beliefs about past experiences must change in order to respond rather than react. In a way, analogous to creating diamonds from coal, deliberate energy must be applied to cause the change. We have practiced old ways of believing and behaving which have become permanent. Practice makes permanent, not perfect. These permanent beliefs and behaviors are known as muscle memory, or "neurological imprints."

For instance, when I believe that anger is wrong, I am trapped. This self-limiting belief keeps me stuck in what have become ineffective, even hurtful, ways of behaving. Change begins by acknowledging the permanence of the old beliefs and behaviors; this muscle memory will not change. What we can and must create is a new belief system in order to have new choices. These choices will lead to new responses, allowing the old beliefs to weaken from lack of use.

Creating this new library of beliefs is a simple yet huge paradigm shift. It is the result of wisdom and insight combined with intellectual, emotional, and experiential awareness. The new belief system allows for reconciliation because we understand that we are powerless to change the past. We are now free to apply our attention, time and energy to new ways of thinking and behaving. Letting go of the belief that we can change the past gives us the freedom to be fully in the present. "Yesterday is history, tomorrow is a mystery, today is a gift, that is why it is called the present."

Creating new beliefs and behaviors is a present to other people as well as us. We no longer have to spend endless time, useless guilt, and needless shame attempting to change our past. What is, *is*! We will now turn the coals of the past into valuable diamonds, gifts of the present.

Reconciliation brings new meaning and value to us and our relationships.

YESTERDAY IS HISTORY, TOMORROW IS A MYSTERY, TODAY IS A GIFT, THAT IS WHY IT IS CALLED THE PRESENT.

Gain from the Pain

Reconciliation is not an easy process. Our anger has caused others and ourselves significant pain. To put the reconciliation process into perspective, we need to appreciate the value we received from the way we dealt with anger in the past. Therefore, we can gain from what has been a painful way of behaving.

Anger has the primary, even primitive, purpose of protecting us. The primary gain is the physical response to fearful external danger, or the fight or flight response. This response prepares our body to handle the potential damage to our physical self. Our bodies respond with an increase in blood pressure and heart rate to more quickly pump oxygen to our muscles. Blood flow is redirected away from the large muscles of the body to limit loss of blood from wounds. Adrenaline is then released to further stimulate our hearts and to focus our attention more completely on the threat. Our breathing rate is heightened to increase our oxygen supply.

THE RECONCILIATION PROCESS RESULTS IN A CONGRUENCE BETWEEN OUR PHYSIOLOGICAL, PSYCHOLOGICAL AND BELIEF SYSTEMS.

Psychologically, our anger helps us to address perceived threats to our self-esteem. As previously written, anger is the guardian of our self-esteem. Our self-esteem is rooted in our belief system. When an outside source threatens our value as a person, our anger rises to protect us, as it must.

The gain we receive from our anger is dramatically increased when our belief system has grown past our negative judgments. Our new belief system clarifies that we are not our anger; therefore, we have the opportunity to choose a response based upon information that reflects value of the other and ourselves. We are then freed from the prison of crooked thinking which, in turn, fuels the courage to change.

The reconciliation process results in a congruence between our physiological, psychological and belief systems. Our broken heart can begin to heal. We can now accept compassion, understanding, persistence, healthy defensiveness, useful denial and purposeful avoidance.

Growing up is a crash course in learning survival skills. Children learn ways to cope by trial and error within a relatively confined space, their family. Through the modeling of parents and others, children are taught what the family deems as acceptable and unacceptable ways of expressing feelings. Children then develop beliefs about love, anger, and disappointment. In fact, all feelings fit into categories as an adolescent: good or bad, positive or negative, acceptable or unacceptable. Therefore, muscle memory and the tendency toward "all or none" thinking begins here. These beliefs help us to survive and fit into our family system.

> CHILDREN LEARNED WAYS TO COPE BY TRIAL AND ERROR WITHIN A RELATIVELY CONFINED SPACE, THEIR FAMILY

The good news is that we as children learn a relatively effective way to get along in our families; the bad news is that what we learn as young individuals is often hurtful and ineffective. Although this system may work within our family, we will face challenges as we develop meaningful relationships outside the home. Differences in goals, expectations and beliefs between us and others will begin to surface. The more apparent these differences become, the more fear, anger, hurt and disappointment are triggered.

Moving past surviving to thriving begins when we move from an all or none thinking model, $R^2 = E/I$ (surrounded by a wounded heart), to a holistic model, $R^1 = I/E$ (surrounded by a healed heart). Assuming the role of a neutral observer allows us to become nonjudgmental and open to receiving new information.

Many of our beliefs are so firmly entrenched that we take them for granted. When an entrenched belief creates negative effects, it's a blind spot. The following questions will help reveal and clarify old beliefs and begin the search for new, more workable beliefs.

Questions:

1. How was my way of dealing with anger as a child helpful to me?

2. What did I take into adulthood from this experience as a child?

3. How does my anger create problems today?

4. Which of these are similar patterns to when I was a child?

5. Which of the following statements keeps me from going beyond surviving to thriving:

   • That's just the way I am.

   • This is who I am; you are not going to change me.

   • Everyone knows I am a hothead.

   • This is just the way God made me.

   • What you see is what you get.

6. What are five of your previous beliefs about anger?

   1. _____

   2. _____

   3. _____

   4. _____

   5. _____

It is imperative that we be proactive in reconciling previous offenses toward ourselves and others. A letter of apology is a beginning step in becoming proactive. There are five essential parts to include in creating an effective apology letter:

1. State the inappropriate behavior briefly and clearly.

2. Acknowledge how the behavior was inappropriate.

3. Acknowledge full and sole responsibility for the behavior.

4. Ask for forgiveness, starting with "Will you forgive me for___."

5. Make restitution (unless doing so causes further harm).

Table 13 helps you create your own apology letter, with your choice of person.

Table 13
Apology Letter

I apologize to...
1. *State the inappropriate behavior briefly and clearly.*
2. *Acknowledge how the behavior was inappropriate.*
3. *Acknowledge full and sole responsibility for the behavior.*
4. *Ask for forgiveness, starting with "Will you forgive me for___."*
5. *Make restitution (unless doing so causes further harm).*

Me

1._____

2._____

3._____

My spouse/significant other

1._____

2._____

3._____

My father/mother

1._____

2._____

3._____

My son/daughter

1._____

2._____

3._____

God

1._____

2._____

3._____

My friend

1._____
2._____
3._____

Other (You know who this is)

1._____
2._____
3._____

RECONCILIATION WITH OTHERS INCLUDES ACCEPTING THAT THE OTHER PERSON MAY NOT RECEIVE YOUR APOLOGY OR DESIRE TO MAKE AMENDS AT THIS TIME.

Reconciliation is a process to make amends and set things right. Reconciliation begins with self and requires a commitment to change old beliefs and accept self-forgiveness. This process follows the principle of love your neighbor as yourself. The key is to love one's self and to love others from a sense of fullness and acceptance.

In most situations others will receive your offer to reconcile, provided it is offered with sincerity and humility. But what happens when the offended party chooses not to reconcile?

Reconciliation with others includes accepting that the other person may not receive your apology or desire to make amends at this time. Your reconciliation efforts could conceivably be rejected. Old beliefs could say, "I made the effort to reconcile and they should receive it." However, you are not in control of the response of others. You have the opportunity to create a new belief system. Unless you create a new belief system, you will remain the victim of your old beliefs, expectations and behaviors.

CHAPTER 6

THE LAW OF INTEGRATION:
"I get to add new beliefs and have more choices."

*I*ntegration is an act or instance of combining into a complete whole, behaving as an individual who is in harmony with the environment, or psychologically organizing the different elements of the personality into a coordinated, harmonious whole.

Integration of the individual is developing congruence between the public, false self and the private, true self. When this connection happens, the public self reflects the idea of being a "10", that is the true self. Integration with the true self is thwarted by crooked thinking that develops from the lies, even partial lies, we have unknowingly received and accepted.

The flaw of integration is that some of our beliefs are based upon blind spots which contain lies that, in turn, lead to disharmony and discord between our thoughts and our feelings. Integration begins by creating a new belief system from of a combination of new and old beliefs. When we unmask the blind spots and question the validity of old beliefs, new beliefs can develop.

As an example, imagine for a moment subjecting a young child to the belief that King Kong is God. Each morning, the child learns to pray to King Kong, thank King Kong for his meals, read about how King Kong created the world, and watch movies about King Kong. There are even statues of King Kong displayed in the home. By the time this child is six or seven years of age, this belief will be firmly entrenched. Even if a child grows up to realize King Kong is a fictional character, his beliefs will not be easily uprooted. Old beliefs remain and continue to influence our choices.

THE CHILD IS LED TO BELIEVE THAT EMOTIONS ARE THE BASIS FOR DISCERNING REALITY FROM FICTION, TRUTHS FROM LIES.

What do Santa Claus, the Easter Bunny and the Tooth Fairy have in common? A FALSE BELIEF! As you read that last sentence, did you experience a little irritation, defensiveness, or perhaps rationalize that it was no big deal? Although these characters may seem innocent in nature, they are still examples of beliefs that contain a lie.

Take this example, another step from a child's perspective. The child whose thinking is black and white and concrete accepts these beliefs as facts. As trite as these examples may seem, the child cannot discern reality from fiction. Since the child has no reason to distrust the influence of his or her caregivers, these beliefs are accepted as true. What does the child learn from these examples? The child is led to believe that emotions are the basis for discerning reality from fiction, truths from lies.

What do we learn from this example? Our decisions are based upon emotions intertwined with false belief. These beliefs are emotionally charged and now must be defended. This is another example of the formula of $R^2 = E/I$, or Reacting = Emotions over Intelligence.

Developing new beliefs requires the new formula, $R^1 = I/E$, Responding = Intelligence over Emotions. As children, we are not able to understand this concept. Old beliefs do remain as we mature, influencing our choices in the present. Developing new beliefs is an intentional exercise which requires diligence, faith, trust in facts, and new experiences to reinforce these facts.

Faith is belief in something not yet seen or experienced. Trust is accepting something as fact not yet seen or experienced. Trust allows us to take action and create a new experience. Every day we have faith that a piece of furniture that looks like a chair will support us when we sit. We trust a new chair will support us even though we may have

FAITH IS BELIEF IN SOMETHING NOT YET SEEN OR EXPERIENCED.

never sat in it before. When we do sit down, this experience becomes evidence which reinforces the belief.

But what if my old belief contains the thought that the leg of the chair has been sawed in half so when I sit down the chair will collapse? If this experience has been engrained for years, I may no longer sit in chairs because I believe that all chairs collapse. It may appear as though the universe is playing a cruel joke and is out to get me; maybe it's other people who are out to get me. Regardless of my thought process, I have created a belief system that keeps me from sitting in chairs due to past negative experiences. Even though I may factually know that not all chairs will collapse, my negative experiences keep me from trusting or having faith in a new experience.

Therefore, trust is a fundamental stepping stone to new experiences. A "new experience" means to go where we have not been before. It also means making decisions without knowing the result. This is a risk. Taking a risk is possible when we trust the competence of our decision-making ability. When the way we're behaving repeatedly doesn't work for us, it is wise to look for unrecognized and/or flawed beliefs.

THE NEW BELIEFS ARE THEN FOUNDED IN TRUTH, BECOMING ANCHORED THROUGH REPEATED NEW EXPERIENCES.

A person needs to have a courageous heart to question old beliefs and search for the truth. We must be willing to let go of old beliefs, however firmly held. Truth always exposes lies. The new beliefs are then founded in truth, becoming anchored through repeated new experiences. This is the process of integration.

Lack of integration affects our lives in many areas. How many people have taken the time to question their heritage, family secrets, religion, or ways they've learned anger? Each of these areas contain emotionally-charged beliefs that may never have been confirmed or challenged, bringing us to an awareness of why we behave as we do. Integration frees us from unwanted actions and their consequences; we do not need to stay prisoners to our learned beliefs.

There are several ways to integrate new beliefs into our thinking. These techniques will affect our behaviors and provide us with new pleasurable outcomes. The following suggestions will help you integrate new patterns to move you toward responding versus reacting.

Beliefs

Look at the word "BELIEFS." Identify how many words you see inside the word "BELIEFS." How many words do you see inside this one word without rearranging the letters?

Is it two or three? Take a look again and see if you can find four words. It is common not to see all four words due to our blind spots.

Which words did you find? Did you see "LIE?" How about "BE?" Most people see these two words right away. It is interesting how so many have believed LIES that keep them from the BE we were created to BE.

BELIEFS ARE THE KEY TO CHANGING OUR BEHAVIORS

Did you see the word "BELIEF?" Sure, now you see it.

The last one, however, is the most difficult one to find and claim: the word "I." How many times did you stare at the word "BELIEFS" and not see the word "I?" Could it BE that you have believed a LIE for so long that your BELIEFS have become immune to evaluation? When the "I" in our beliefs is denied or undervalued, it will affect our life's journey. BELIEFS are the key to changing our behaviors.

Claiming who you are, your "I" or true self, is the new foundation of your being. When you stay anchored in this new belief about yourself, you are able to claim that "I am more than my anger." Even if your behavior occasionally displays inappropriate reactions, there is a new anchor point. Your behavior no longer defines you; you are more than your anger. You can change unwanted behavior by first changing the belief that has directed the anger.

Give yourself permission to fail forward as you integrate this new belief into your life. Outside influences may say things like, "You haven't changed. You are still an angry woman (or man). That workshop, book or counselor didn't make any difference for you at all." Or, relax. When these comments come, and they will, remember to refer back to your new beliefs. Claim who you are and add the word "YET" to your vocabulary: "I may revert back at times, but that is not who I am. I am not there *yet*, but I am working on it."

Train Thoughts

The following illustration clarifies this process:

Imagine a three car-length train. There is an engine, a fuel car and a caboose. The engine represents the "facts", the fuel car represents the "faith" we put into our decisions, and the caboose represents our "feelings." When the train of life is being led by the caboose, we are being led by our Reactions – $R^2 = E/I$; our feelings are directing our choices.

When the formula is reversed to Response $R^1 = I/E$, our feelings are subjected to our intellect. This act requires an understanding of what kind of fuel is in the fuel car. Is the information you are receiving based upon emotional experiences or reality? When feelings do arise, it is important not dismiss them. They need to be validated as an indication that something is happening within me. Feelings are a prompt, so remember to ask yourself:

- What is my expectation?
- What information do I have concerning this event or adversity that is taking place?
- Do I need more information?
- What are my expectations?
- Is this a possible blind spot?

- Should I contact an accountability friend to process what is going on?

Fueling your train with these types of questions will lead you toward the engine of facts. Once you have the facts, you are more equipped to make a decision. Sometimes these decisions may still require "faith," especially if that decision involves a new experience.

As an example, Jim comes home after a difficult day at work to find that, once again, his eight-year-old son has left his bicycle in front of the garage. For reasons of stress, expectations and beliefs, Jim begins to fume: "I have told him over and over again, not to leave his bike there! Why didn't his mother correct him? Don't they care about what I want?"

Clearly, Jim's emotions of frustration, impatience and hurt will prompt him to lash out at his son or wife as he enters the house. This scene illustrates the formula $R^2 = E/I$, reacting equals emotions over intelligence. Emotions, the caboose, have directed his choice in reacting to the event. Notice that Jim has not considered all of the facts.

In order to put intelligence over feeling, Jim must become aware of his beliefs through self-examination, coaching or an experiential workshop like the *Heart of the Courageous*. Using his intelligence, the engine of the train, Jim would be able to consider other facts. "I'm stressed out and need to relax" or "My son is only eight." The new choice becomes, "I will deal with this when I am in a better frame of mind." Over time, as Jim becomes more practiced, he will use his feelings as a stepping stone to search out the facts. Perhaps his son's bike shows evidence of an accident. Yet, even if there was no accident, Jim could ask himself what would be the most effective way to teach his son about his bike.

Muscle Memory

We have found muscle memory to be a helpful metaphor. Muscle memory is the concept that when an action is repeated, over time that action is more easily repeated. Muscle memory changes the old adage "practice makes perfect" to "practice makes permanent". What we do is repeatedly reinforced and becomes second nature, a habit. Changing old habits requires intent and repetition. A clue that we are on the right track is the feeling of discomfort when old habits resist change.

Neuroscience calls this concept "Neuro-Linguistic Programming" or NLP. NLP shows that our thoughts, emotions and experiences combine to direct what is inscribed in our highest brain center, the cerebral cortex. The effect of NLP on the brain is similar to the way CDs and DVDs are made. Mental data is inscribed on a disc and provides the same recording each time it is played. This data becomes muscle memory. This phenomenon, Neurological Associative Conditioning (NAC) is the result of NLP; NAC determines our belief system.

CHANGING OLD HABITS REQUIRES INTENT AND REPETITION.

Our belief system is analogous to a garden, which might be a combination of weeds and flowers. The weeds represent learned and hurtful beliefs. The flowers represent learned and helpful beliefs. Sometimes a garden is overrun by weeds. Pulling up the weeds is a waste of energy and time. It would appear at first glance that they have been eliminated; yet, many times the weed breaks off, leaving the root to grow again. A more effective approach is to supersaturate the garden with flowers, the new-helpful beliefs.

Some beliefs contain a partial truth and a partial lie. For example, if you grew up being told you were an angry boy or an angry girl, you might believe this is true. What is the partial truth? I am a boy or girl. What is the partial lie? I am an "angry" boy or "angry" girl. The truth is I am a boy or girl who is angry. Many beliefs require scrutiny to expose a fallacy.

Integration Tools

Revisit the feelings exercise.

Retake the feelings exercise (Table 3) to identify your most recent feelings. After you have identified these feelings, go back to each word and apply the $R^1 = I/E$ formula. Validate each feeling. Then, identify the expectation or underlying fact that leads to the feeling. This exercise will create new muscle memory.

Deep Breathing

Deep breathing affects the system in a similar way to an increase in oxytocin. Oxytocin, as mentioned earlier, has the effect of buffering the impact of adrenaline.

BREATHING IS A USEFUL DAILY EXERCISE THAT MODERATES THE EFFECT OF THE ADRENALINE CREATED BY THE STRESS IN OUR LIVES.

Breathing is a useful daily exercise that moderates the effect of the adrenaline created by the stress in our lives. Allowing time to breathe deeply is also useful in acute situations when we feel overwhelmed with anger; it will quickly change our emotional state.

Take a slow deep breath from your abdomen through your nose. Hold this breath for the count of 20 to 24. Exhale slowly through your mouth for a count of 10 to 12. Repeat this action 10 times in the morning, afternoon and evening. You may find for the first few days that your chest may feel stretched and possibly sore; this is normal since your lungs are a muscle. The breathing exercise will help change your emotional state by countering the effect of adrenaline.

Wind in the Sail

When we are confronted with something that tends to ruffle our feathers, a helpful response is considered purposeful avoidance. Like a sailboat, when the wind of an unpleasant event starts, we can raise the sail to catch the wind or leave it down and minimize its effect. If I raise my sail to catch the wind, I enhance the influence of the wind. If I recognize that the situation is unhelpful, it would be wise to leave the sail down. When someone challenges me, I have the choice to purposefully avoid the challenge. This can be a simple response like, "Right now is not a good time to talk about this. I would prefer to address this issue at another time." Keep it simple. You don't have to react; you get to respond.

> YOU DON'T HAVE TO REACT; YOU GET TO RESPOND.

Bulldog with No Teeth

Imagine you are walking down the sidewalk with a friend and suddenly a ferocious barking bulldog is running toward you. Fear sets in and you are paralyzed. The bulldog's large mouth grabs your leg and you start screaming in pain. To your surprise, your friend starts laughing at you and almost falls to the ground. You're hurt by your friend's reaction, yet you realize there really isn't any pain.

Your friend, still laughing, points to the bulldog and cries out: "The bulldog is toothless! The best he can do is gum you to death!" When you look down, you realize that the bulldog really *is* toothless and really *can't* hurt you. So it is with many false beliefs that we have stored in our muscle memory. When time is taken to reflect upon the facts, in many cases, the situation is not as it "feels" to be.

Humor, a Merry Medicine

Humor has a way of lightening up life's adversities. Learning to laugh at times of struggle is healthy. Not everything in life is laughable, yet many times we can find a way to see the humor in a circumstance. The willingness to look for the humor will help create humor. Think of the saying, "Well, they can't eat me!" In other words, "What is the worst that can happen?" This doesn't mean you should be cynical or sarcastic but rather witty and practical. Remember the bulldog example? Can you see the bulldog gumming your leg? So you got a little leg massage on your way to the supermarket. Maybe you'll have to wash your jeans. The good news is the incident didn't cost you a dime, just a little anxiety. Now, you can have a good ole belly laugh. Maybe next week, you could bring a new friend along the same path. This time they can be "bitten" and you can have the laugh.

Although this example is a bit extreme, it does direct you to a new way of looking at the events that happen to you. What if there are no accidents? What if you choose to look for the humor in life?

Here are some of the effects of having humor in our lives:
- Cuts stress in half by reducing the stress hormone cortisol
- Lowers blood pressure
- Increases energy
- Promotes happiness and joy

- Stimulates the immune system
- Promotes healing physically and emotionally
- Fosters a positive attitude
- Promotes social flexibility
- Increases the "feel good" chemicals, or endorphins [16]

Humor has been called "social glue" because it bonds us to one another and reduces social conflict. Humor is the most overlooked, under-prescribed, and inexpensive therapy available.

There are many ways to bring humor into your life. You could read a humorous book or watch a funny movie. The internet also opens up endless possibilities. Learn to tell jokes or look for humor even in yourself.

---

[16] Melinda Smith, M.A., Gina Kemp, M.A., and Jeanne Segal PhD., "Laughter is the Best Medicine", May 2010.

CHAPTER 7

THE LAW OF CO-CREATION:

"I will let go of the outcome and trust the process."

*T*he *"Law of Co-Creation" emphasizes our need to accept help.* This help is available to us in resources other than ourselves, including other people, experiential workshops, books, prayer, meditation, and certainly, God. Accepting help is critical for change. We are not meant to do life alone.

This book has described new ways of thinking and behaving that can be powerful when utilized. It may be enticing to believe "If I learn all I need to know, I will be able to stop the problems I create with my anger." Again, head knowledge will not lead the way to change. It simply does not work for long-term transformation.

Looking at this erroneous belief more closely, we see the truth and the lie. The truth is that learning about blind spots, styles of anger, beliefs and past experiences provides a foundation for change – but not the change itself. It is tempting to believe the lie that all you need is more information to make changes. In fact, no matter how much new information you have, blind spots will continue to cause you to hit barriers. You cannot see your own blind spots without the help of God and others.

Acknowledging the need for help allows for feedback, support and the experience of changing. There is little in this life that you can actually control or change. You cannot control what another person thinks, says, feels or does. You cannot even control your own feelings! Therefore, you cannot control the results of your choices no matter how well intentioned those choices might be.

FAITH CAN BE DEFINED AS THE BELIEF IN THINGS WE HAVE NOT SEEN OR EXPERIENCED, YET CAN BE SEEN AND EXPERIENCED IN THE LIVES OF OTHERS.

You might ask yourself, "If there is so much that I do not control, how do I live with all of the uncertainty that this creates?" The only conclusion is *faith*! Faith can be defined as the belief in things we have not seen or experienced. While this definition may appear subjective, it is difficult to argue with the objective changes others described having seen in us.

The authors' faith journey grew as they realized the fallacy of attempting to control themselves or the outcome; Control just didn't work. The following passage reveals an experience through finding faith:

In 1996, Gary accepted that he needed help after over-reacting in an angry confrontation with my spouse. The situation led him to seek professional help where he received suggestions that included an emphasis on gaining new information through advice and books. Although there was some benefit from these suggestions, the angry behavior did not change; information and will power alone did not lead to lasting change. Gary's blind spots remained undetected and his behavior continued to be filled with anger, rage and unrecognized toxic shame. When he finally confided in Harry about his difficulty in changing behaviors a new door opened that allowed Gary to be accepted without judgment.

The authors created a relationship based on trust, respect and compassion. This connection allowed both to be vulnerable without being judged, truthful without being shamed and encouraged without efforts to be "fixed." Regardless of stumbling blocks, the relationship provided a new foundation for change based on faith and hope. They also found that an attitude of "failing forward" gave them the opportunity to experience healthy and continuing changes. They were able to develop love-based anger to replace the defensive anger of pain, fear and shame. This process of faith confirmed their belief that we need help beyond ourselves.

THIS CONNECTION ALLOWED BOTH TO BE VULNERABLE WITHOUT BEING JUDGED, TRUTHFUL WITHOUT BEING SHAMED AND ENCOURAGED WITHOUT EFFORTS TO BE "FIXED."

Co-creating with God

As co-authors who have searched and researched, we have concluded there is a power greater than ourselves. We have found that this power can and will help us make the changes that we alone cannot make, even with the best of help and intention. For us this power is God, who is an infinite and personal God. He is an infinite God in that He goes beyond our abilities and is, therefore, greater than ourselves. He is personal in that He is concerned about and empathizes with each one of us.

As accountability partners, we were able to help each other confront our various beliefs about religion and spirituality. Many beliefs are rooted simply in culture, family of origin, and hurtful experiences. Many other beliefs were contaminated with prejudices, black or white thinking, fear, toxic shame and even outright lies. Emotional and spiritual abuse often leads to a distorted view of God. Each one of us needs to face and ultimately set aside our former beliefs about God, taking the position of a dispassionate newspaper reporter to examine our beliefs objectively.

> WE TOOK THE POSITION OF A DISPASSIONATE NEWSPAPER REPORTER TO EXAMINE OUR BELIEFS ABOUT GOD.

It is not the authors' intent to impose their beliefs upon you, the reader. Yet it is well worth the time and patience to examine your spiritual beliefs, along with other beliefs of the past, as part of the healing process; this step in self-exploration can often be a catalyst for change.

Our Faith Journey

We, Gary and Harry, have already given you pertinent and helpful information which we know can be beneficial to you. We encourage you to continue your search with an open mind and a vulnerable heart.

Our weekly meetings confirmed the belief that a spiritual foundation is the basis for peace of mind, emotional and physical well-being, and a personal sense of significance. The meetings also established our belief that we are spiritual beings on a physical journey. Restoring our wounded heart allows us to return to a child-like faith of acceptance of God, ourselves and others. We can then let go of a need to be in control and reach up, much like a child does to a loving father or mother. Aligning with the belief that there is a personal and infinite God who accepts and loves us as we are is the essence of co-creating.

Co-creating with Mankind

...ACCEPTANCE PRECEDES TRANSFORMATION

We believe co-creating with mankind is an extension of co-creating with God. Our faith strengthened as we worked together. As our faith increased, we became more trusting of the potential for growth in all of our relationships. Developing partnerships is essential to continued growth.

The Importance of an Accountability Partner

Other people can provide support, encouragement and feedback regarding blind spots. Remember, we cannot see our own blind spots. An accountability partner provides a safe, trusting and encouraging ally. We have met twice a week for over six years and continue to do so. We continue to share, validate and challenge one another about our beliefs, blind spots and self-defeating, nonproductive behavior. By listening without judgment and eliminating advice, we became open to creating a workshop for others to experience similar growth and change. We recreated our process in a group setting. Hundreds of other people began to experience what we had experienced. The workshop extended the concept of an "accountability partner" or "anger ally" into a group setting.

As stories were shared in the workshops, the participants felt hope and excitement. They knew that their honesty was not being judged. Allowing one another to share painful experiences and validate feelings created hope and acceptance. They became aware that acceptance precedes transformation. The participants learned that they are more than their anger and inappropriate behaviors. They began to recognize that who we are is more important than what we do. To know who we are frees us from proving who we are. Inappropriate behaviors are never excusable; recognizing that these unwanted behaviors can and will change your response to adversity.

> TO KNOW WHO WE ARE FREES US FROM PROVING WHO WE ARE.

Guidelines for an Accountability Partnership

The following are some suggestions we used for sharing with an accountability partner:

1. Be clear with one another that accountability is personal and private.
2. Find ways to see the value even in the most painful events.
3. Remind each other that just because I *feel* attacked does not mean that I *am* attacked.
4. Transparency in the relationship is essential and involves full disclosure of our regrettable words and behaviors.
5. Accountability involves ownership without blame. It is open discussion of efforts to change and asks the question, "What could I have done differently?"
6. No judgments!

CHAPTER 8

Conclusion

*W*e *want to honor you for your courage* and desire to change! We believe what you have read will be a helpful foundation for those changes. Remember, knowing who we are frees us from proving who we are; we may not always feel like a 10, yet the fact remains we are a 10.

As humans, we have an inborn nature to seek pleasure and avoid pain. Logic and experience tell us that growth demands a willingness to seek change, regardless of delayed pleasure or present difficulty. There may be times when your best efforts do not result in change. One or more of the following may be a contributor:

- Unrecognized blind spots
- Unidentified addiction
- Unrecognized clinical problem, such as anxiety or depression
- Previous physical trauma to the brain
- Chemical imbalance

To resolve any doubts consider professional help.

The experience of changing is a commitment to finding and changing our blind spots and the beliefs that support them. It is a process of removing barriers to our passion, creativity and spiritual growth. It is also the recognition that process does not always look like progress. Sometimes, it will be one step forward and two steps backward. Other times, it will be failing forward and getting back up and trying again. You may feel knocked down, but you are not knocked out.

Discouragement is the enemy of growth. We will always become discouraged when we feed old beliefs that trigger anger, criticism, and "the black wolf" of shame. We spend needless energy attempting to eradicate old beliefs that keep us stuck in self-defeating behaviors. Directing our energy toward beliefs that are affirming and "the white wolf" of support, leads to heartfelt encouragement and lasting change. Accepting the beliefs that I can change, and I will change, creates the opportunity for change.

Our story has been a journey over the last six years that includes the good, the bad, and the ugly. We have sustained our relationship and changed our beliefs and behaviors. We have been privileged to see hundreds of men and women discover and write their own new story. We trust that, through diligence and faith, you will also turn the coals of the past into the diamonds of the present.

APPENDIX

Table 1
Evaluation Form

Check all the areas that applied in the past or still apply today:

___I raise my voice when I get upset, irritated or angry.
___I may yell occasionally.
___I occasionally swear.
___I have raged but not always.
___I pout.
___I numb out.
___I shut down inside and remain quiet.
___I avoid further discussions.
___I make sarcastic comments.
___I steam on the inside and bite my tongue.
___I stare or look away.
___I change the subject or abruptly leave.
___I attack the other person.
___I may start an argument or even a fight.
___I defend myself and tell the other person that they are wrong.
___I do whatever it takes to calm the other person down.
___I get afraid.
___I feel hurt and disrespected.
___If in bed and I feel angry, I will turn my back on my partner and make it clear that they are on the outside.
___On the inside I hope that my partner will take some initiative but when they don't it drives my hurt even deeper.
___I tell the other person that they have issues and they need some help.
___I threaten to leave the house.
___I leave and don't mention when I will be back.
___I threaten by saying things like, I am moving out, or mention the "D" word.
___I cut off love and communication for hours and sometimes even days.
___I go read a self-help book on how to fix the situation.
___I call a friend and tell them how awful my partner has been to me.
___I wonder what others will think if they knew we fought and got angry.
___I throw things or sometimes break things.
___I have been known to be physically abusive and hit someone.
___I get angrier when I drink alcohol.
___I medicate myself in other ways when I get angry.
___I have been in trouble with the law because of my anger.
___I take my anger out on other people who are not part of the problem.
___I get angry and then try to fix it by being nice.
___I do not tell even a close friend about my problems from anger.
___I try to please to prevent conflict with my partner.
___I feel sad or depressed when there is a conflict.
___I stuff my feelings.
___I sometimes have thoughts of revenge.

Table 2
What's Not Working?

⊗ *Check the areas that currently apply in your everyday life.*

⊛ *Circle the areas that were once not working but now are working.*

○ Career   ○ Intimacy

○ Marriage   ○ Sex life

○ Relationship   ○ Thought life

○ Children   ○ Housing accommodations

○ Fear/anxiety   ○ Divorce

○ Parents   ○ Divorce pending

○ Siblings   ○ Raising kids alone

○ Sickness   ○ Blending families

○ Stress   ○ Dating

○ Financial pressures   ○ Loss of power

○ Relationship with God   ○ Restless

○ Anger/frustration   ○ Financial success

○ My weight   ○ Time pressures

○ Too much time on my hands   ○ Church/Synagogue

○ Eating   ○ Exercise

○ Control/Controlled   ○ Procrastination

Table 3
Feelings

Circle the words that describe how you are feeling. Move quickly through the words checklist without thinking them. In essence, don't think your feelings, just feel them.

☐	☐		☐	☐		☐	☐
apprehensive	reverence		rage	infuriated		bummed	melancholy
terror	doubtful		furious	irritated		depressed	gloomy
leery	inadequate		angry	accosted		sorrow	dismay
uneasy	scared		enraged	indignant		downcast	mournful
anxiety	awe		hot	pissed		low	shameful
frightened	paranoid		hostile	fury		discontent	timid
panic	alarmed		uptight	resentment		woeful	disappointed
spooked	skeptical		inflamed	irate		uncertain	unhappy
fearful	afraid		annoyed	wrath		failure	regret
mistrust			upset	provoked		dejected	blue
afraid			animosity			brooding	somber
horror			mad			worried	helpless

☐	☐		☐	☐		☐	☐
powerless	weak		vengeance	animosity		down	overpowered
dependent	incompetent		bitter	bitterness		overtaken	pushed
lost	crippled		hostile	envy		captive	tyrannized
exhausted	resourceless		disfavor	detest		misused	used
feeble	spent		dislike	loathing		trampled	crossed
vulnerable	abandoned		adverse	despise		trodden	mistreated
defenseless	inefficient		abhorance	disaffection		afflicted	subdued
destitute	depleted		hateful			burdened	pressured
impotent			spite			crushed	
defeated			resentment			persecuted	

☐	☐		☐	☐		☐	☐
failure	unsatisfied		happy	glad		loving	adulation
unfulfilled	discouraged		gaiety	mirth		passion	admiration
discontent			freaked-out	jazzed		desiring	affectionate
disillusioned			mellow	pleasure		concern	adoring
disenchanted			exuberant	turned-on		appreciation	empathy
failed			jubilant	elated		rejoiceful	togetherness
downcast			terrific	contentment		caring	
unhappy			elation	triumphant		befriended	
let-down			spirited	wonderful		infatuation	

Now, write the following words in the large boxes above (left to right):
Fear, Anger, Sadness, Powerlessness, Hate, Oppression, Disappointment, Joy, Love

Write the total number of circled feelings for each category in the small boxes. Below, total the number of love and joy feelings, non-love and non-joy feelings, and all feelings.

Love & Joy	
Non-Love & Joy	
Total	

Adapted from Dr. Linda L. Moore's book *Release from Powerlessness*

Table 4
Evidence of Repression

Do you repress your anger? **Check** *the following statements that apply:*

- ☐ When I get angry, I don't get over it.
- ☐ I feel frustrated, disappointed or irritable much of the time, but I just don't ever get angry.
- ☐ I am sarcastic or cynical about myself, others, or the world around me.
- ☐ I often go overboard with my teasing.
- ☐ I am depressed frequently for long periods of time.
- ☐ I seem to get angry all of the time.
- ☐ I feel powerless about my life.
- ☐ I feel guilty when I get angry.
- ☐ I feel ashamed when I get angry.
- ☐ I withdraw or remove myself emotionally when I am hurt or angry.

Table 5
10 Styles of Anger

Explosive

Predictable: Grenade or IED

1. Sudden anger (impulsive, immediate)

2. Shame-based anger (hidden, poor self-image)

3. Deliberate anger (calculated, planned)

4. Addictive anger (self-fulfilling)

Unpredictable is Predictable: Long Fuse or Gotcha

5. Habitual anger (learned, repeated)

6. Moral anger (judgmental, self-righteous)

7. Hate (hardened resentment)

Implosive

Unpredictable: Camouflaged

8. Anger avoidance (denial, stuffing)

9. Sneaky anger (silent aggression)

10. Paranoid anger (hyper-suspicious)

Table 6
Anger Quiz

Check the boxes next to the statements that apply to you:

- ☐ 1. I try to never get angry.
- ☐ 2. I get really nervous when others are angry.
- ☐ 3. I feel I'm doing something bad when I get angry.
- ☐ 4. I tell people I'll do what they want, but then I often forget.
- ☐ 5. I say things like, "Yeah, but..." and "I'll do it later."
- ☐ 6. People tell me I must be angry, but I'm not sure why.
- ☐ 7. I get jealous a lot, even when there is no reason.
- ☐ 8. I don't trust people very much.
- ☐ 9. Sometimes it feels like people are out to get me.
- ☐ 10. My anger comes on really fast.
- ☐ 11. I act before I think when I get angry.
- ☐ 12. My anger goes away very quickly after I explode.
- ☐ 13. I get very angry when people criticize me.
- ☐ 14. People say I am easily hurt and oversensitive.
- ☐ 15. I get angry when I feel bad about myself.
- ☐ 16. I get mad in order to get my way.
- ☐ 17. I try to scare others with my anger.
- ☐ 18. I can pretend to be very mad when I'm really OK.
- ☐ 19. Sometimes I get angry just for the excitement or action.
- ☐ 20. I like the strong feelings that come with my anger.
- ☐ 21. My anger takes over and I go out of control.
- ☐ 22. I seem to get angry all the time.
- ☐ 23. I just can't break the habit of getting angry a lot.
- ☐ 24. I get mad without thinking—it just happens.
- ☐ 25. I become very angry when I defend my beliefs and opinions.
- ☐ 26. I feel outraged about what others try to get away with.
- ☐ 27. I always know I'm right in an argument.
- ☐ 28. I hang onto my anger for a long time.
- ☐ 29. I have a hard time forgiving people.
- ☐ 30. I hate people for what they've done to me.

Total the number of statements that applied to you from each group of three questions

Questions	Total that apply	Anger Style
1-3	_____	Anger Avoidance
4-6	_____	Sneaky Anger
7-9	_____	Paranoid Anger
10-12	_____	Sudden Anger
13-15	_____	Shame-based Anger
16-18	_____	Deliberate Anger
19-21	_____	Addictive Anger
22-24	_____	Habitual Anger
25-27	_____	Moral Anger
28-30	_____	Hate

Table 7
The Drama Triangle

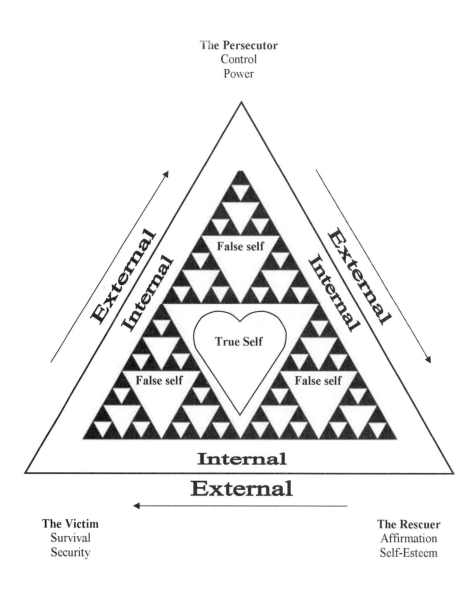

The Persecutor
Control
Power

False self

True Self

False self   False self

External

Internal

External

Internal

Internal

External

The Victim
Survival
Security

The Rescuer
Affirmation
Self-Esteem

The common thread of each role is **MANIPULATION.**

Table 8
Discovering Your Roles in the Drama Triangles

Reflect on and answer the following questions:

1. When and how was I victimized as a child?

2. When and how was I a rescuer as a child?

3. When and how was I a persecutor as a child?

4. When and how was I victimized as an adult?

5. When and how was I a rescuer as an adult?

6. When and how was I a persecutor as an adult?

Table 9
Twenty-one Lessons Learned About Anger

1. Everyone has anger.

2. Anger is an emotion.

3. Emotions, like colors, are not right or wrong.

4. Emotions need to be validated not obeyed.

5. Anger is the guardian of our self-esteem.

6. I am not my anger.

7. Everyone uses repression.

8. Repression can be hurtful or helpful.

9. What we don't know can hurt ourselves and others.

10. Repression causes our blind spots.

11. Repression is responsible for the creation of our false self.

12. The mask of defensiveness that we wear is our false self.

13. The cost of our masks is the loss of intimacy with us and others.

14. Removing our masks reveals our true selves.

15. Our true self is a 10.

16. There are two types and ten styles of anger.

17. Implosive anger is as destructive as explosive anger.

18. My feeling of anger and my angry behavior are separate.

19. My anger styles were modeled for me.

20. Anger is either LOVE-BASED or FEAR-BASED.

21. Anger is a GIFT.

Table 10
Miller and Rahe Stress Scale

Work through Miller and Rahe's list of life events. Score your "life change units" for events you have experienced in the last year. Afterwards, total your score.

Life Event	Life Change Units	Your Score
Major change in health or behavior of family member	55	
Marriage	50	
Pregnancy	67	
Miscarriage or abortion	65	
Gain of a new family member:		
Birth of a child	66	
Adoption of a child	65	
A relative moving in with you	59	
Spouse beginning or ending work	46	
Child leaving home:		
To attend college	41	
Due to marriage	41	
For other reasons	45	
Change in arguments with spouse	50	
In-law problems	38	
Change in marital status of parents:		
Divorce	59	
Remarriage	50	
Separation from spouse:		
Due to work	53	
Due to marital problems	76	
Divorce	96	
Birth of grandchild	43	
Death of spouse	119	
Death of other family member:		
Child	123	
Brother or sister	102	
Parent	100	

Personal and social:		
Change in personal habits	26	
Beginning or ending school or college	38	
Change of school or college	35	
Change in political beliefs	24	
Change in religious beliefs	29	
Change in social activity	27	
Vacation	24	
New, close, personal relationship	37	
Engagement to marry	45	
Girlfriend of boyfriend problems	39	
Sexual difficulties	44	
"Falling out" of close personal relationship	47	
An accident	48	
Minor violation of the law	20	
Being held in jail	75	
Death of a close friend	70	
Major decision regarding your immediate future	51	
Major personal achievement	36	
Financial:		
Major change in finances		
Increased income	38	
Decreased income	60	
Investment and/or credit difficulties	56	
Lost or damaged personal property	43	
Moderate purchase	20	
Major purchase	37	
Foreclosure or mortgage or loan	58	
Total		

Score of 450+: Worrisome
Score of 301-450: Fair
Score of 150-300: Good
Score 150-: Excellent

Table 11
Anger Received and Given

○ *Find a quiet place where you can be alone. Begin thinking about your life following the directions below.*

○ *Think about one person in your life with whom you have received and given anger. In the form below, answer the questions about this person's interaction with you.*

○ *Then, think about* **at least, but not limited to, 10** *instances of receiving and giving anger involving significant people in your life. Browse through the sample list of people and issues in Table 12 to help you identify those relationships, or create your own.*

○ *Be specific. Be clear. Be honest.*

○ *If more space is needed, feel free to use an extra sheet.*

○ *Remember, you will only get out of this what you put into it.*

Write Name of Person/Issue _____

Anger Received

What did this person do or say? Anger you received as a child, teenager or adult:

_____
_____
_____

What did it do to you?

_____
_____
_____

Anger Given

What did you do or say? Anger you gave to this person:

_____
_____
_____

What did it do to him/her?

_____
_____
_____

What did you lose because of this anger?

_____
_____
_____

How does this affect you today?

_____
_____
_____

137

Table 12
List of Choices of Anger Received/Given

Father	Step-Father	Mother
Step-Mother	Grandfather	Grandmother
Foster Parent	Guardian	Spouse/Partner
Ex-Spouse/Partner	Ex-Boyfriend/ Girlfriend/ Fiancé	Father/Mother of your child
Your child/children	Step-child/children	Sibling(s)
Boss	Co-worker	Teacher
Classmate	Friend	Don't know who they are
Other relationship	Pornography	Abuse (sexual/emotional/ mental/verbal)
Alcohol	Drugs	God

Table 13
Apology Letter

I apologize to…

1. *State the inappropriate behavior briefly and clearly.*
2. *Acknowledge how the behavior was inappropriate.*
3. *Acknowledge full and sole responsibility for the behavior.*
4. *Ask for forgiveness, starting with "Will you forgive me for___."*
5. *Make restitution (unless doing so causes further harm).*

Me

1. _____
2. _____
3. _____

My spouse/significant other

1. _____
2. _____
3. _____

My father/mother

1. _____
2. _____
3. _____

My son/daughter

1. _____
2. _____
3. _____

God

1. _____
2. _____
3. _____

My friend

1. _____
2. _____
3. _____

Other (You know who this is)

1. _____
2. _____
3. _____

BIBLIOGRAPHY

Arterburn, Stephen and David Stoop. *Boiling Point: Understanding Men and Anger.* Nashville: W Publishing Group, 1991.

Bradshaw, John. *Healing the Shame That Binds You.* Deerfield Beach: Health Communications, Inc., 1988.

Bradshaw, John. *Homecoming: Reclaiming and Championing Your Inner Child.* New York: Bantam Books, 1990.

Carter, Les, Ph.D. and Frank Minirth, M.D. *The Anger Workbook: A 13-step Interactive plan to help you...*Nashville: Thomas Nelson Publishers, 1993.

DeFoore, William Gray, Ph.D. *Anger: Deal with it, Heal with it, Stop it from Killing You.* Deerfield Beach: Health Communications, Inc., 1991.

Ellis, Albert Ph.D. *Anger: How to Live with and without it.* New York: Citadel Press, 1977.

Fisher, Robert. *The Knight in Rusty Armor.* Chatsworth, CA: Wilshire Book Company, 1990.

Gospic K, Mohlin E, Fransson P, Petrovic P, Johannesson M, et al. (2011) *Limbic Justice—Amygdala Involvement in Immediate Rejection in the Ultimatum Game.* PLoS Biol 9(5): e1001054. doi:10.1371/journal.pbio.1001054

Grad, Marcia. *The Princess Who Believed in Fairy Tales.* Chatsworth, CA: Wilshire Book Company, 1995.

Harbin, Thomas J. Ph.D. *Beyond Anger: A Guide for Men.* New York: Marlowe & Company, 2000.

Hegstrom, Paul, Ph.D. *Angry Men and the Women Who Love Them.* Kansas City: Beacon Hill Press of Kansas City, 1999, 2004.

Kuzmich, Gary and Wayne McKamie. *The Passionate Heroic Zone,* Oahu, Hawaii: Watermark Publishing Company, 2006.

LaHaye, Tim and Bob Phillips. *Anger is a Choice.* Grand Rapids: Zondervan, 1982.

Lerner, Harriet, Ph.D. *The Dance of Anger: A Woman's Guide to Changing the Patterns of Intimate Relationships.* New York: Harper Perennial, 1985.

Miller, M and Rahe, R.H. *Life Changes Scaling for the 1990s.* Journal of Psychosomatic Research, 43:279-292, 1997.

Moore, Linda, Ed.D. *Release from Powerlessness,* Dubuque, Iowa: Kendall/Hunt Publishing Company, 2004.

Oliver, Gary, Ph.D. and H. Norman Wright. *Good Women Get Angry: A Woman's Guide to Handling Anger, Depression, Anxiety and Stress.* Ann Arbor: Vine Books, 1995.

Potter-Efron M.S.W., Ron and Pat Potter-Efron, M.S. *Letting Go of Anger: The 10 Most Common Anger Styles and What to Do About Them.* N.p.: Barnes & Noble Books, 1995.

Powers, Marcia. *The Dragon Slayer with a Heavy Heart.* Chatsworth, CA: Wilshire Book Company, 2003.

Semmelroth, Carl, Ph.D. *The Anger Habit in Relationships.* Naperville, IL: Sourcebooks, Inc., 2005.

Tavris, Carol. *Anger: The Misunderstood Emotion.* New York: Touchstone Book, 1982.

Whitfield, Charles L., M.D. *Healing the Child Within.* Deerfield Beach: Health Communications, Inc., 1987.

Williams, Redford, M.D. and Virginia, Ph.D. *Anger Kills: Seventeen Strategies for Controlling the Hostility That Can Harm Your Health.* New York: Harper Perennial, 1984.

Wilson, David Sloan. *Fairness Research* in New York Times, p. D2, 7/5/2011.